THE ULTIMATE
DERBY
QUIZ BOOK

THE ULTIMATE
DERBY
QUIZ BOOK

Compiled by Chris Cowlin
Forewords by Jim Smith and Marco Gabbiadini

APEX PUBLISHING LTD

First published in hardback in 2009

Apex Publishing Ltd

PO Box 7086, Clacton on Sea, Essex, CO15 5WN, England

www.apexpublishing.co.uk

British Library Cataloguing-in-Publication Data
A catalogue record for this book
is available from the British Library

ISBN: 1-906358-36-2   978-1-906358-36-5

Typeset in 10.5pt Chianti Bdlt Win95BT

Cover Design: Siobhan Smith

Printed in Great Britain by the MPG Books Group, Bodmin and King's Lynn

Author's Note:
Please can you contact me: **ChrisCowlin@btconnect.com** if you find any mistakes/errors in this book as I would like to put them right on any future reprints of this book. I would also like to hear from Derby County fans who have enjoyed the test! For more information on me and my books please look at: **www.ChrisCowlin.com**

This book is in no way officially associated with Derby County Football Club, it is unofficial and unauthorised.

I would like to dedicate this book to:

My daughter - baby 'Sophie Olivia Cowlin',
13 February 2009 - sadly missed by all the family.

FOREWORD

The time I spent as manager of Derby County was amongst the happiest of my footballing career. The fans were superb and we enjoyed some great matches and goals together. It is a fantastic club with a great history and hopefully a great future.

Highlights include 'that' Paolo Wanchope goal, the win over Manchester United and winning promotion into the Premier League. We made progress in each of our first three seasons at the top level and I thoroughly enjoyed every moment of my time at the club.

Having attempted to answer the questions in this book I have been reminded of some of the fantastic moments from Derby County's past. I even managed to answer most of the questions about me! I can see that it is a book which Derby fans of all ages are going to enjoy and I'm sure it will be a challenge for even the most committed Rams supporter.

Enjoy the book and the memories!

Jim Smith
Derby County Football Club (Manager 1995-2001)

FOREWORD

I am honoured to have been asked to write the foreword to Chris Cowlin's 'The Ultimate Derby Quiz Book'.

I arrived from Crystal Palace in January 1992 after Arthur Cox signed me to join the Rams for £1 million. I played with some great players during my time at the club and played under three different managers. I was delighted to win the player of the season award in my first full season at the club and I made 188 League appearances, scoring 50 goals. It was a great moment in my career playing in the top-flight, Premier League football with Derby County during 1996/1997, which of course was my last season at the club – I would advise you to remember these facts as they will help when you are answering the Marco Gabbiadini section!

The history of Derby County is long and varied and I'm sure the questions included in this book will bring back plenty of memories.

Having been fortunate enough to see a preview of this book, I know that Derby County fans of all ages will be entertained for hours with questions about the Rams past and present.

As the club continues to write new chapters in the Club's history, it's always fitting to remember what went before.

I hope you all enjoy this wonderful quiz book as much as I did.

Marco Gabbiadini
Derby County Football Club (1992-1997)

INTRODUCTION

I would first of all like to thank Jim Smith and Marco Gabbiadini for writing the forewords to this book. I am very grateful for their help on this project and was truly delighted when they agreed to write a few words. I would also like to thank all the local newspapers and radio stations for their comments and reviews (which can be found at the back of the book).

I really hope you enjoy this book. Hopefully it should bring back some wonderful memories of this fantastic club! I am sure the great Brian Clough would have liked to test his knowledge on this great football club.

In closing, I would like to thank all my friends and family for encouraging me to complete this project.

Chris Cowlin.

Best wishes
Chris Cowlin

For more information on the author please see:

www.ChrisCowlin.com

CLUB RECORDS AND HISTORY

1. In which year was the club formed – 1884, 1886 or 1888?

2. What is the club's nickname?

3. The club's record attendance of 33,072 at Pride Park was recorded in March 2008 against which team whilst playing in the Premier League?

4. Which 15-year-old became the club's youngest ever player in 2002 whilst playing against Grimsby Town?

5. Who became the club's most expensive player in 2007, costing £3.5 million from Norwich City?

6. Can you name the two years that the club won the Division One title in their history?

7. How many times have the club won the FA Cup in their history?

8. In which year did the club move to Pride Park?

9. Which trophy did the club win during July 2007 when they beat Nottingham Forest 2-0 at Pride Park?

10. Which player holds the record for appearing the most times for Derby County, playing 589 games in all competitions, scoring 201 goals?

ROY McFARLAND

11. In which position did Roy play during his playing days?

12. In which season did Roy captain the club to the Division Two Championship?

13. Which managers made Roy their second signing for Derby County in 1967?

14. Against which country did Roy make his England debut in February 1971?

15. How many League goals did Roy score in his Derby career – 34, 44 or 54?

16. Against which team did Roy score for Derby in a 1-1 away draw on the opening day of the 1968/1969 season?

17. Which team did Derby play on Boxing Day 1972 in a 3-1 home win, with Roy scoring a brace in the game?

18. How many League appearances did Roy make for Derby County in his career – 442, 542 or 642?

19. During the 1980/1981 season, Roy became the fifth, sixth or seventh player to play in more than 500 League games for County?

20. How many League goals did Roy score for Derby County during 1973/1974 in 38 starts?

NATIONALITIES – 1

Match the player to his nationality

21.	Paulo Wanchope	Scottish
22.	Mark Pembridge	Croatian
23.	Taribo West	Trinidad & Tobago
24.	Paul Peschisolido	Costa Rican
25.	Craig Burley	Welsh
26.	Aljosa Asanovic	English
27.	Deon Burton	Croatian
28.	Peter Shilton	Canadian
29.	Stern John	Jamaican
30.	Igor Stimac	Nigerian

MARCO GABBIADINI

31. In which year was Marco born on 20 January – 1966, 1967 or 1968?

32. How much did Arthur Cox pay for Marco in January 1992 to bring him to the Baseball Ground?

33. Against which team did Marco score his debut goal for Derby County on 1 February 1992?

34. How many League goals did Marco score for Derby in his first season at the club, in his 20 starts?

35. Against which Essex based team did Marco score a brace in a 7-0 home win in the League Cup 2nd round, 2nd leg during October 1992?

36. Against which team did Marco score a League hat-trick during January 1994 in a 4-0 home win?

37. How many League goals did Marco score in Derby's promotion season, 1995/1996, in his 33 starts and six substitute appearances?

38. True or false: Marco scored in three League games during December 1995 and Derby County won all three matches?

39. How many Premier League appearances did Marco make in his Derby County career, all during the 1996/1997 season – 14, 24 or 34?

40. Against which team did Marco score a brace in the 2-2 away draw during December 1993?

NICKNAMES – 1

Match the player to his nickname

41.	Mr T	Marco Gabbiadini
42.	Cat	Geraint Williams
43.	Banana	Grzegorz Rasiak
44.	Sticks	Francesco Baiano
45.	Rodders	Tom Huddlestone
46.	The Pie Man	Chris Powell
47.	Ray	Deon Burton
48.	Banjo Boy	Gordon Cowans
49.	Sid	Ian Ormondroyd
50.	Leaky Bun	Gary Charles

DIVISION THREE NORTH CHAMPIONS – 1956/1957

51. Which team finished four points behind The Rams in second place?

52. How many of Derby's 46 League games did they win – 24, 25 or 26?

53. Which manager led the club to this success?

54. Which team did Derby beat 5-3 at home on the opening day of the League season?

55. Which player finished the club's highest League scorer with 37 goals in 44 matches?

56. True or false: Derby beat Chesterfield 7-1 in the home League game during April 1957?

57. True or false: Four Derby County players played in every League game during the season?

58. Which team did the Rams play at home on Christmas day and then again away on Boxing Day, winning both matches, 4-0 at home and 4-1 away?

59. In how many of the clubs 46 League matches did Derby County fail to score a goal?

60. True or false: Derby was unbeaten in the League during their five matches during March 1957?

DEAN STURRIDGE

61.   In which position did Dean play during his playing days?

62.   In which year was Dean born in Birmingham – 1971, 1972 or 1973?

63.   Which Rams manager handed Dean his League debut for Derby?

64.   Following on from the previous question, can you name the Essex based team Dean made his League debut against during January 1992?

65.   How many League goals did Dean score for The Rams during 1995/1996?

66.   Against which team did Dean score a brace on the opening day of the 1996/1997 season in a 3-3 home draw?

67.   Which team did Dean sign for when he left Derby County in 2001?

68.   Against which team did Dean score the winning goal away from home in a 2-1 win during May 1997, Gary Rowett scored the other for Derby?

69.   Which London team did Dean score against both at home and away during the 1999/2000 season?

70.   Against which team did Dean score his last Derby League goal, in a 2-2 away draw during August 2000?

STADIUMS

71.   What is the name of County's current stadium?

72.   Following on from the previous question, what is the capacity of the stadium – 31,597, 32,597 or 33,597?

73.   Following on from the previous question, in which year did the team move to the new stadium, opened by The Queen?

74.   Following on from the previous question, which team did Derby play in their first League game, only for the game to be abandoned due to floodlight failure?

75.   True or false: Derby County played Premier League football whilst at the Baseball Ground?

76.   In which year did the club move to the Baseball Ground?

77.   Which stand in the Baseball Ground was damaged due to a German air raid in January 1941?

78.   Which London club were the final opponents at the Baseball Ground in a League match in a 3-1 defeat with Derby player Ashley Ward scoring the club's last ever League goal in the stadium?

79.   In January 2009, which former legend had a bust unveiled, which is located next to the home dugout?

80.   What is the postcode of Derby's current stadium?

MANAGERS

*Match the manager to the year he took over
at Derby County*

81.	Dave Mackey	2003
82.	Billy Davies	1995
83.	Colin Murphy	2002
84.	Arthur Cox	1973
85.	John Gregory	1962
86.	Paul Jewell	1976
87.	Colin Addison	2006
88.	George Burley	2007
89.	Tim Ward	1979
90.	Jim Smith	1984

ROY CARROLL

91.   In which tear was Roy born – 1976, 1977 or 1978?

92.   In which position does Roy play?

93.   In which year did Roy sign for Derby County from
       Glasgow Rangers?

94.   Against which team did Roy make his Derby County
       debut in a 1-1 away draw with Emanuel Villa scoring
       Derby's equaliser in the 89th minute?

95.   How many League games did Roy play in for Derby
       County in his first season at the club?

96.   Which London club did Roy play for between 2005 and
       2007?

97.   What nationality is Roy, also having won full
       international caps for his county?

98.   Which team signed Roy from Wigan Athletic in July
       2001?

99.   True or false: Roy once scored a League goal for Hull
       City in his career?

100.   Which Rams manager signed Roy and handed him his
       debut for Derby County?

COLIN BOULTON

101. In which position did Colin play during his playing days?

102. In what year was Colin born in Cheltenham – 1945, 1955 or 1965?

103. Which manager signed Colin for Derby County?

104. What is Colin's middle name?

105. In how many of Derby's 42 League games during 1971/1972 did he keep a clean sheet?

106. Can you name the two seasons that Colin won a Division One Championship medal with Derby County?

107. True or false: Colin once scored a League goal for Derby County in his career?

108. How many League appearances did Colin make in his Derby County career – 272, 273 or 274?

109. True or false: In Colin's first season at the club he made six League appearances for Derby County and the club lost five of them?

110. Colin played in all 42 League matches during 1974/1975, can you name the only other Rams player to play in all of Derby's matches throughout the season?

DIVISION ONE CHAMPIONS – 1971/1972

111. Which Yorkshire team finished one point behind Derby to finish second?

112. Following on from the previous question, can you name the other two sides that also finished one point behind County, finishing in third and fourth places?

113. Which manager led the club to this success?

114. Who was Derby's Player of the Season?

115. Who scored the only goal to win the championship for Derby against Liverpool at home on the final day of the League season during May 1972?

116. Who finished the club's highest League scorer with 15 goals?

117. How many players were used during Derby's 42 League matches – 16, 20 or 24?

118. Which team were the first side to beat Derby by 1-0 during October 1971, having been undefeated in the League for the first 12 matches?

119. Who scored Derby's only goal in the 1-0 win against Chelsea at home on New Year's Day 1972?

120. Who scored the club's first League goal of the season in a 2-2 home draw against Manchester United on the opening day of the season?

PLAYER OF THE YEAR – 1

Match up the player to the year he won the title

121.	2005/2006	Charlie George
122.	2003/2004	Ted McMinn
123.	2001/2002	Ron Webster
124.	1993/1994	Tommy Smith
125.	1991/1992	Roy McFarland
126.	1989/1990	Youl Mawene
127.	1975/1976	Danny Higginbottom
128.	1973/1974	Colin Todd
129.	1971/1972	Mark Wright
130.	1968/1969	Martin Taylor

DERBY V NOTTINGHAM FOREST

131. Which striker scored County's equaliser in the 1-1 home League match during November 2008?

132. How many times did the clubs meet during the 1960s?

133. Which Poland striker scored a brace for Derby in the 3-0 home League win in the Championship against Forest during December 2004?

134. Which team finished higher in the League in Division One during 2003/2004?

135. What was the score in the club's first ever Premier League meeting during October 1996 at the City Ground?

136. Who scored County's only goal in the 1-0 home win against Forest during April 1999?

137. True or false: The clubs didn't meet in any competition during the 1940s?

138. What was the score when Derby played Forest at the Baseball Ground in Division One during February 1972?

139. Which team finished higher in the League in Division One during 1988/1989?

140. Which forward scored a brace for Derby in the 4-2 home League win against Forest during March 2004, with Ian Taylor and Marcus Tudgay scoring the other goals for The Rams?

SQUAD NUMBERS – 2008/2009

Match up the player with his Derby County squad number

141.	Robbie Savage	32
142.	Jordan Stewart	16
143.	Rob Hulse	8
144.	Andy Todd	4
145.	Mohammed Camara	11
146.	Darren Powell	5
147.	Paul Connolly	22
148.	Mile Sterjovski	17
149.	Dean Leacock	2
150.	Paul Green	30

SPONSORS

Match up the company to the year in which they became the club's shirt sponsors

151.	Derbyshire Building Society	1986
152.	Bass Brewers	1980
153.	Bombardier	1998
154.	Auto Windscreens	1984
155.	EDS	2005
156.	Puma	1992
157.	Patrick	2001
158.	British Midland	1995
159.	Marston's Pedigree	2008
160.	Sportsweek	1981

STEVE BLOOMER

161. How many playing spells at Derby County did Steve have during his football career?

162. In which year did Steve captain Derby County to the Division Two Championship?

163. Against which team did Steve make his Rams debut during September 1892?

164. How many League appearances did Steve make for Derby County is his career – 474, 475 or 476?

165. In which position did Steve play during his playing days?

166. How many League goals did Steve score for Derby County is his career – 293, 295 or 297?

167. Which team did Steve join in 1906 only to return four years later?

168. How many of County's nine goals did Steve score in the 9-0 home win against Sheffield Wednesday during January 1899?

169. How many full England caps did Steve win for his country – 21, 22 or 23?

170. True or false: Steve scored more goals than the number of appearances he made for England at full international level?

WHERE DID THEY GO – 1

Match up the player to the team he joined after leaving Derby County

171.	Craig Fagan	Tottenham Hotspur
172.	Paulo Wanchope	Stoke City
173.	Robert Earnshaw	Napoli
174.	Dean Yates	Dundee
175.	Andy Griffin	West Ham United
176.	Christian Dailly	Watford
177.	Grzegorz Rasiak	Nottingham Forest
178.	Aljosa Asanovic	West Ham United
179.	Fabrizio Ravanelli	Hull City
180.	Rob Lee	Blackburn Rovers

WHO AM I? – 1

181. I was born in 1973 and my middle name is Constantine, I made my debut for the Rams in January 1992 against Southend United. I left Pride Park in 2001 and joined Wolves.

182. I was the club's Player of the Season for 1980/1981, I was a goalkeeper and joined the Rams in 1980 from Stoke City.

183. I was the only Derby player to play in all 42 League matches during the 1958/1959 season.

184. I managed the club during the 1946/1947 season.

185. I played for Derby between 1998 and 2002, I am Argentinean and cost Jim Smith £3 million when I signed for the Rams.

186. I was Derby's record transfer costing £1.375 million in 1991, I scored 30 League goals for the Rams in my career.

187. I played in goal for Derby, Harry Storer signed me for the Rams costing £6,300. I made a total of 225 League appearances for Derby County in my career.

188. I played for the Rams as a wing half or full back, I was born in 1934 and was a part of the team that won the Division Three North championship in the 1956/1957 season.

189. I joined Derby from Watford in 2008. I was born in Birmingham in 1982 and my first professional club was Leicester City.

190. I am a striker and signed for the Rams in 2008 from Sheffield United, I have also played for Crewe, West Bromwich Albion and Leeds United.

1960s

191. Who was Derby's manager during the 1961/1962 season?

192. What was the score in Derby's last League game of this decade, a game at home to West Bromwich Albion on 27 December 1969?

193. Which midfielder did The Rams sign in August 1968 from Sheffield United for £60,000?

194. Who was the club's highest League scorer during 1967/1968 with 21 goals?

195. Which season was Tim Ward's last as Derby manager during the 1960s?

196. In which division were The Rams playing during 1962/1963?

197. Who became the club's record signing, paying nearly £40,000 for him in September 1966?

198. True or false: The club lost six of the opening seven League matches at the start of the 1965/1966 season?

199. Can you name the goalkeeper who played in all 42 League games during 1963/1964?

200. Which Derby player became the third player in the club's history to play in 500 appearances for The Rams during April 1965 against Ipswich Town at the Baseball Ground?

NICKNAMES – 2

Match the player to his nickname

201.	Ace	Lee Morris
202.	Solly	Jacob Laursen
203.	Choppy	Seth Johnson
204.	Bazooka	Paulo Wanchope
205.	Jug Ears	Leighton James
206.	Parsley	Aljosa Asanovic
207.	Brooklyn	John O'Hare
208.	Sethlad	Horacio Carbonari
209.	Cracker	Rory Delap
210.	Taffy	Mel Sage

WHERE DID THEY COME FROM – 1

Match the player to the club he joined Derby County from

211.	Paul Connolly	Portsmouth
212.	Paul McGrath	Ipswich Town
213.	Terry Hennessey	Plymouth Argyle
214.	Gary Rowett	Nottingham Forest
215.	Russell Hoult	Sheffield United
216.	Lewis Price	Aston Villa
217.	Rob Hulse	Everton
218.	Rory Delap	Leicester City
219.	Alan Stubbs	Everton
220.	Deon Burton	Carlisle United

1970s

221. Derby won the Division One Championship during the 1971/1972 season, but which position in the League did they finish the following season – third, fifth or seventh?

222. Which team did Derby beat 8-2 at home in Division One during October 1976?

223. Can you name the three players that all scored twice in the 6-2 away win on the last day of the 1975/1976 season against Ipswich Town in April 1976?

224. Which Derby player was appointed Scotland captain in May 1976 against England, the first Rams player to do so in the club's history?

225. How many matches did Derby lose out of their 46 League games during their 1971/1972 League Championship success – six, seven or eight?

226. Which Rams player won the Player of the Season award during the 1973/1974 season?

227. Which Derby manager sold Charlie George to Southampton during December 1978?

228. Against which team did Derby record their biggest League win of the 1978/1979 season, a 4-1 home in during November 1978?

229. Which Derby player was the first to score five goals in a competitive game since Hughie Gallacher in 1934, in a 5-0 home win against Luton Town during March 1975?

230. Which Rams player won the Player of the Season award during the 1977/1978 season?

2008/2009

231. In which month during the season did Nigel Clough take over at Pride Park as Derby County manager?

232. Against which team did Derby record their first League win in the Championship, their League game of the season, at home during September 2008?

233. Can you name the team Derby beat 2-1 at home on 31 January 2009, this being Nigel Clough's first win in the League as Derby manager?

234. Can you name the three goalscorers for Derby in the 3-1 home League win against Norwich City during October 2008?

235. Which Danish defender did Derby sign in July 2008 from West Bromwich Albion on a free transfer?

236. Which striker scored the only goal for the Rams in the 1-0 home League win against Watford during December 2008?

237. With which club did Derby share a 1-1 away draw during August 2008, for the Rams to pick up their first point of the League season?

238. Who scored Derby's two goals, including a last minute equaliser against Charlton Athletic in the 2-2 away draw during December 2008?

239. Which forward wore the number 11 squad number during this season?

240. True or false: Derby beat Norwich both at home and away in the League fixtures?

FOUR OR FIVE GOALS IN A GAME

241. Which striker scored four goals for Derby against Cesena in the Anglo-Italian Cup during September 1994 in a 6-1 home win?

242. Who is the only player in the clubs history to score 6 goals in a competitive game, against Sheffield Wednesday during January 1899?

243. Who scored four goals for Derby County against Tottenham Hotspur during October 1976 in Division One?

244. True or false: Jack Bowers once scored four goals in five different competitive matches for Derby County in the 1930s?

245. What was the score when Alan Hinton scored four goals against Stockport County in the League Cup 2nd round at home during September 1968?

246. Which competition were Derby County playing in when Alf Ackerman scored four goals in a 6-2 home win during April 1956 against Accrington Stanley?

247. Who was the first person to score five goals in a competitive game for Derby County in December 1889 against Aston Villa in a 5-0 home win?

248. Which competition were Derby County playing in when Jack Stamps scored four goals in a 4-1 home win during September 1950 against Blackpool?

249. True or false: So far in Derby County's history, a Derby County player has scored four goals in one or more matches during every decade since being formed?

250. Who scored five goals for Derby County against Luton Town during March 1975 in Division One at home?

LEAGUE APPEARANCES – 1

Match the player to the number of League appearances
he made for Derby County

251.	Frank Wignall	19 (8)
252.	John Robertson	47 (9)
253.	Ian Ashbee	88
254.	Lars Bohinen	2 (1)
255.	Taribo West	90 (26)
256.	Nigel Callaghan	1
257.	Eric Steele	72
258.	Mark Stallard	29 (16)
259.	John Sims	18
260.	Malcolm Christie	47

ALAN HINTON

261. Where did Alan play on the field – in the middle, on the left or on the right?

262. In which year was Alan born in Wednesbury – 1941, 1942 or 1943?

263. How much did Alan cost the Rams when he was signed for the club?

264. Following on from the previous question, in which year was Alan signed for Derby County during September?

265. Against which team did Alan make his Derby League debut in a 4-1 home win?

266. How many League goals did Alan score in his first season at Derby?

267. Against which East Anglian team did Alan score a brace in the 3-1 home win during August 1969?

268. How many League appearances did Alan make in his Derby County career – 243, 253 or 263?

269. How many League goals did Alan score for Derby during 1971/1972 in his 38 starts?

270. Against which team did Alan score a brace in the 3-2 home win during April 1971?

EUROPEAN CUP

271. In which year did Derby first compete in this competition?

272. Which player scored a brace in the 2-0 home win in the 3rd round, 2nd leg against the Czechoslovakian team Spartak Trnava in March 1973?

273. Can you name the two managers who have been in charge on the two occasions Derby have been in this competition?

274. True or false: Derby County has won this competition on one occasion?

275. Which Spanish giants beat The Rams 6-5 on aggregate after extra time in the 2nd round of the competition during October and November 1975?

276. Can you name the only player in the club's history to score a hat-trick in a European Cup match?

277. Can you name the goalkeeper who has played in all 12 European matches for Derby County in their history?

278. What is Derby's record win in this competition against Real Madrid?

279. Which Italian team beat Derby in the semi-final of the 1972/1973 competition 3-1 on aggregate?

280. Which Yugoslavian team were the opponents in the club's first ever European match?

281. True or false: Not one Derby County player played in all 38 League matches?

282. Which French defender scored the only goal in the 1-0 home win against Southampton during November 2001?

283. Which two players both finished the season with nine League goals?

284. Against which club did Derby County record their only League win of the season during March 2002, a 3-1 win away from home?

285. Which team did Derby County draw 1-1 with on the final day of the League season away from home?

286. Which midfielder scored the only goal in the 1-0 home win against Tottenham during February 2002?

287. How many managers did the club have during this season?

288. Following on from the previous question, can you name them?

289. How many points did Derby County finish with in the League, finishing in 19th place?

290. Which Italian striker scored County's first goal of the season on the opening day in a 2-1 home win against Blackburn Rovers?

HONOURS

Match up the title to the year Derby County were placed

291.	FA Cup Winners	1975
292.	Charity Shield Winners	1972
293.	Division One Champions	2007
294.	Anglo-Italian Cup Runners-Up	1946
295.	Championship Play-Off Winners	1903
296.	Division One Runners-Up	1971
297.	FA Cup Runners-Up	1993
298.	Texaco Cup Winners	1975
299.	Watney Cup Winners	1936
300.	Division One Champions	1972

NATIONALITIES – 2

Match the player to his nationality

301.	Lars Bohinen	American
302.	Branko Strupar	Republic of Ireland
303.	Grzegorz Rasiak	Norwegian
304.	Marino Rahmberg	Israeli
305.	Rory Delap	Estonian
306.	John Harkes	Swedish
307.	Avi Nimni	Belgian
308.	Jacob Laursen	Finnish
309.	Mart Poom	Danish
310.	Simo Valakari	Polish

DIVISION ONE RUNNERS-UP – 1995/1996

311. How many points behind were Derby County from the Champions Sunderland?

312. Which manager guided the club to this success?

313. Which striker finished County's highest League scorer with 20 goals in 33 starts and six substitute appearances?

314. True or false: Derby County won all five League matches during December 1995?

315. Against which team did Derby County record their highest win of the season, a 6-2 home win during April 1996?

316. Following on from the previous question, who scored a hat-trick in the game?

317. How many of the club's 46 League matches did they win – 19, 20 or 21?

318. Against which team did Derby County record their first League win of the season, in their fifth League match in a 2-1 win away from home?

319. Which East Anglian team did Derby beat 2-1 on New Year's Day 1996 at home with Ron Willems and Gabbiadini scoring the goals for The Rams?

320. Can you name County's two goalkeepers who played in all 46 League matches, one started 40 matches and the other six?

NIGEL CLOUGH

321. True or false: Nigel played for Manchester City during his career?

322. How many full England caps did Nigel win for his country – 4, 14 or 24?

323. Against which London club did Nigel manage his first Derby County League match, during January 2009 in a 2-0 home defeat?

324. Which club did Nigel join from Nottingham Forest in 1993?

325. In which year was Nigel born in Sunderland – 1965, 1966 or 1967?

326. What is Nigel's middle name – Harry, Howard or Harvey?

327. Which team did Nigel join in 1998 as player/manager, this was also the club he joined Derby County from in 2009?

328. Which Derby County manager did Nigel take over from in January 2009?

329. Can you name the two years that Nigel won a League Cup winners medal?

330. Which team knocked Derby out of the League Cup in the 2008/2009 semi-finals in Nigel's second match in charge at the club, beating Derby 4-3 on aggregate?

BRIAN CLOUGH

331. In which year was Brian appointed Derby County manager with Peter Taylor?

332. What was the first trophy that Derby County won when Brian was in charge at the Baseball Ground?

333. Which player did Brian sign in 1972 and became a British record signing, costing £225,000?

334. Where was Brian born in March 1935?

335. True or false: Brian won full international caps for England?

336. In which position did Brian play during his playing days?

337. Which team did Brian manage before retiring in 1993?

338. As well as winning the Division One Championship and the Central League, which Cup did Derby win with Brian in charge as manager during 1971/1972?

339. Which team did Brian go on to manage when he left Derby County as manager?

340. Which round of the 1972/1973 European Cup did Derby County reach with Brian in charge before getting knocked out by Italian side Juventus?

DIVISION ONE CHAMPIONS – 1974/1975

341.   Which manager guided the club to this success?

342.   Which team did Derby play on the last day of the League season, ending in a 0-0 draw at home during April 1975?

343.   How many of the club's 42 League matches did they win?

344.   Can you name the two clubs that finished two points behind Derby, finishing in 2nd and 3rd places with 51 points?

345.   Who was the club's Player of the Season?

346.   Can you name one of the two players who played in every League game this season?

347.   True or false: The club won all six League matches during March 1975?

348.   Which team did Derby County beat 2-0 at home in their third match of the season, the club's first League win of the season?

349.   Who scored a hat-trick in the 5-2 home win during November 1974 against Queens Park Rangers?

350.   Who finished the club's highest League scorer with 15 goals?

LEAGUE GOALSCORERS – 1

Match the player to the number of League goals he scored for Derby County

351.	Luciano Zavagno	7
352.	Ray Swallow	100
353.	Marcus Tudgay	42
354.	George Thornewell	82
355.	Jack Stamps	17
356.	Jackie Whitehouse	15
357.	Igor Stimac	23
358.	Frank Wignall	21
359.	Dean Saunders	3
360.	Marco Reich	3

TOMMY JOHNSON

361. In which year was Tommy born – 1969, 1970 or 1971?

362. How much did Derby County pay for Tommy, a then club record - £1.275 million, £1.375 million or £1.475 million?

363. Against which team did Tommy score the winning goal in the 2-1 home win during the final day of the 1991/1992 season during May 1992?

364. How many League goals did Tommy score for the Rams during 1992/1993?

365. Which Derby manager bought Tommy and handed him his Rams debut?

366. Against which team did Tommy score a brace for Derby County during November 1994 in a 2-0 home win?

367. Which Midlands club did Tommy sign for when he left Derby County?

368. How many League appearances did Tommy make for Derby County in his career – 88, 98 or 108?

369. How many England Under-21 caps did Tommy win, scoring two goals?

370. At which club did Tommy start his football career?

THE FA CUP

371. Which Derby midfielder scored the Rams winner in the 4-3 away win during January 2009 in the 3rd round against Forest Green Rovers?

372. Which Derby player scored a hat-trick in the 6-1 home win in the 2nd round during December 1985 against Telford United?

373. Which team ended Derby's run in the semi-finals during April 1976, the match being played at Hillsborough?

374. Which Derby player scored a hat-trick in the 6-1 away win in the 3rd round replay during January 1974 against Boston United?

375. Can you name the three years that the club were runners up in this competition?

376. True or false: Derby went out of this competition in the 3rd round on seven occasions in the 1980s?

377. Which Midlands based club did Derby beat 3-1 at home in the 4th round during January 1997?

378. Which team did Derby beat 4-2 on penalties after a 2-2 home draw and a 1-1 away draw in the replay during January 2008?

379. Which London team did Derby beat 4-1 in the 1946 FA Cup Final at Wembley Stadium?

380. Following on from the previous question, can you name the Derby player who scored a brace in the game?

BRUCE RIOCH

381. Against which team did Bruce score his first League goal of the 1974/1975 season, in a 3-2 away defeat during September 1974?

382. How many League goals did Bruce score for Derby County during his two spells at the club, making a total of 146 starts and one substitute appearance – 28, 38 or 48?

383. Against which team did Bruce score a brace in Derby's FA Cup quarter-final 4-2 home win during March 1976?

384. How many goals did Bruce score whilst being ever present in the 1974/1975 League season – 15, 16 or 17?

385. Against which East Anglian based team did Bruce make his Derby League debut in a 4-2 away win during February 1974?

386. In what position did Bruce commonly play – defender, midfielder or striker?

387. How many full international caps did Bruce win for his country, scoring six goals – 14, 24 or 34?

388. True or false: Bruce has managed Derby County in his managerial career?

389. How much did Bruce cost The Rams when he signed from Aston Villa in February 1974?

390. Following on from the previous question, which Derby manager signed Bruce for the club?

DEAN SAUNDERS

391. True or false: Dean became Derby's first £1 million signing in the club's history when he signed for The Rams?

392. Against which club did Dean make his Derby League debut scoring a brace in the 4-1 home win during October 1988?

393. Which Derby manager signed Dean for The Rams?

394. How many League goals did Dean score in his first season at the Baseball Ground in his 30 starts?

395. Against which team did Dean score a hat-trick for Derby in the 5-0 League Cup 2nd round second leg win during October 1989?

396. Against which team did Dean score his last Derby League goal during May 1991 in a 3-2 home defeat?

397. How many League goals did Dean score for Derby County in his 106 appearances in his career – 42, 45 or 48?

398. Which team did Dean sign for when he left the Baseball Ground for £2.9 million?

399. Against which team did Dean score a hat-trick for Derby in the 6-2 League win during May 1991?

400. True or false: Dean was the only Derby player to play in all 38 League matches during 1990/1991?

PLAYER OF THE YEAR – 2

Match up the player to the year he won the title

401.	2004/2005	Francesco Baiano
402.	2000/2001	Michael Forsyth
403.	1999/2000	Steve Cherry
404.	1997/1998	Bobby Davison
405.	1990/1991	Mart Poom
406.	1987/1988	Steve Buckley
407.	1984/1985	Chris Riggott
408.	1982/1983	Inigo Idiakez
409.	1979/1980	Dave Mackay
410.	1970/1971	Dean Saunders

PETER SHILTON

411. How many League appearances did Peter make for Derby in his football career?

412. From which team did Peter join Derby County in 1987?

413. Against which team did Peter make his Derby League debut in a 1-0 home win during August 1987?

414. How many full England caps did Peter win for his country – 120, 125 or 130?

415. True or false: Peter played in all 40 of the club's League matches during his first season at the Baseball Ground?

416. Which Rams manager signed Peter for Derby County?

417. In which position did Peter play during his playing days?

418. What is Peter's middle name – Leslie, Lloyd or Lionel?

419. Which team did Peter manage between 1992 and 1995?

420. How old was Peter when he made the last of his 1,005 League appearances in his career, whilst playing for Leyton Orient?

COLIN TODD

421. From which team did Brian Clough sign Colin in 1971 for Derby County?

422. In which season did Colin win the Derby County Player of the Year?

423. In which position did Colin commonly play for The Rams?

424. In which season did Colin manage Derby between Jim Smith at the start of the season and John Gregory at the end of the season?

425. Which award did Colin win in 1975?

426. How many England caps did Colin win for his country?

427. Against which club did Colin make his Derby League debut in February 1971 in a 2-0 home win?

428. How many League goals did Colin score in the 1971/1972 season at the Baseball Ground?

429. Which team did Colin sign for when he left Derby County in 1998?

430. In which year was Colin born – 1947, 1948 or 1949?

LEGENDS

Rearrange the letters to reveal the name of a club legend

431. YHNER TNNWOE

432. CAJK SLAINCHO

433. GGEREO NLLIOC

434. OLNIC DDTO

435. YAR GUNOY

436. ERG RSIANROH

437. UALP NSPMSIO

438. TEERP NAEIDL

439. RAGY MIEHKICLTWE

440. LLBI RRCUY

FRANCIS LEE

441. Which Rams manager signed Francis for Derby County?

442. Which team did Francis play for before joining Derby County in 1974?

443. Following on from the previous question, how much did Derby pay for Francis?

444. Against which team did Francis make his Derby County debut in a 0-0 away draw on the opening day of the 1974/1975 season?

445. True or false: Francis scored his first Rams goal on his home League debut, his second League match in his Derby County career?

446. How many League goals did Francis score for Derby in his 28 starts during 1975/1976?

447. Against which team did Francis score a brace in the 2-2 home draw during April 1976?

448. In which position did Francis play during this playing career?

449. Against which team did Francis score a brace in the 2-1 away win during October 1974?

450. Francis won 27 full international caps for England, but how many goals did he score – 8, 10 or 12?

MIDDLE NAMES

Match the player to his middle name

451.	Peter Doherty	Leslie
452.	Charlie Morris	Prescott
453.	Bruce Rioch	Richard
454.	Darryl Powell	Derrick
455.	David Nish	Henry
456.	Reg Matthews	David
457.	John McGovern	Aylmer
458.	Roy McFarland	Dermont
459.	Peter Daniel	John
460.	Francis Lee	Anthony

THE CHAMPIONSHIP PLAY-OFF WINNERS – 2006/2007

461. Which team did Derby beat in the play-off final at Wembley?

462. What was the score in the play-off final?

463. Who scored County's winning goal in the play-off final?

464. Who played in goal for Derby County in the play-off final?

465. What was the attendance in the play-off final – 74,993, 75,993 or 76,993?

466. Which team did Derby County beat in the play-off semi-finals, finishing 4-4 on aggregate and then beating them 4-3 on penalties?

467. Which manager guided Derby County to this success?

468. In which position did Derby County finish in the Championship to reach the play-offs?

469. Following on from the previous question, how many points were Derby County away from finishing in second place to be automatically promoted?

470. Which Yorkshire team did Derby County beat 2-0 at Pride Park on the final day of the League season during May 2007?

PLAYER POSITIONS

*Match the player to the position he played
in at Derby County*

471.	Paul Connolly	Midfielder
472.	Simon Coleman	Striker
473.	Georgiou Kinkladze	Defender
474.	Adam Bolder	Goalkeeper
475.	Rob Hulse	Defender
476.	Igor Stimac	Midfielder
477.	Mile Sterjovski	Defender
478.	Cyril Fox	Midfielder
479.	Brian Launders	Striker
480.	Liam Dickinson	Midfielder

1980s

481. In which position in the League did Derby finish in Division One during 1988/1989?

482. How many of the club's 42 League matches did they win during 1981/1982?

483. Which Derby player finished the club's highest League scorer during 1981/1982 with nine goals in 20 starts and four substitute appearances?

484. Who won the Derby Player of the Year award in both the 1988/1989 and 1989/1990 seasons?

485. Who scored a hat-trick for Derby in the 3-0 home win during April 1984 against Crystal Palace in Division Two?

486. In which year in the 1980s did chairman Robert Maxwell take over at the club?

487. Who scored Derby's only goal in the 1-0 home win on the opening day of the 1987/1988 League season against Luton Town?

488. Who was the first person since Kevin Hector in the 1967/1968 season to score 20 League goals or more in a season, this was achieved during the 1984/1985 season scoring 24 League goals in 46 League appearances?

489. What did Derby achieve during the 1985/1986, the first Third Division club to achieve this?

490. Which manager took over from Colin Addison when he left the club in January 1982?

WHO AM I? – 2

491. I was a striker at the club and once played 106 consecutive appearances from October 1988 to May 1991.

492. I am a full Scotland international and signed for the Rams in 2008 from Nottingham Forest.

493. I played a total of 486 League appearances for Derby County in my career, scoring 155 goals.

494. I was the first player to score a European Cup goal for Derby County in their history in September 1972.

495. I was appointed Derby manager in June 2005. I later took Hull City to the Premier League, their first ever season in top flight football.

496. I was a striker, born in Nottingham and scored 50 League goals for Derby in my career. I left the club in 1996.

497. I was born in 1980, I am a defender who signed for the club in 2008 from West Bromwich Albion, I am capped at full international level for Denmark.

498. I was born in Derby in 1980 and started my professional football career at Derby County. I left Pride Park in 2003 and joined Middlesbrough.

499. Dave Mackay signed me for Derby County in 1973, I was born in Wales in 1947, I was a defender, my previous club was Swindon Town.

500. I hold the club record for scoring the most League goals for Derby County with 293 goals in my 474 appearances. I also scored a record 18 hat-tricks in my time at the club in all competitions.

WHERE DID THEY COME FROM – 2

Match the player to the club he joined Derby County from

501.	Eddie Lewis	Manchester United
502.	Paul Boertien	Newcastle United
503.	Kenny Miller	Leeds United
504.	Branko Strupar	Fulham
505.	Matt Oakley	Manchester United
506.	Craig Short	Carlisle United
507.	Dean Leacock	Genk
508.	Danny Higginbotham	Southampton
509.	David Jones	Celtic
510.	Warren Barton	Notts County

2007/2008

511. Who started the season as manger of the Rams before Paul Jewell took over as Derby County manger in November 2007?

512. Which Welsh midfielder did the club sign from Blackburn Rovers in January 2008

513. How many of the club's 38 League matches did they win - 1, 11 or 21?

514. With which team did Derby share a 0-0 draw at Pride Park on the opening day of the League season?

515. Against which club did The Rams record a 1-0 home win during September 2007?

516. Following on from the previous question, can you name the Derby goalscorer in the game?

517. Can you name the club's two goalscorers in the 2-2 away draw against Newcastle United on 23 December 2007?

518. Which Derby player scored the club's goal in the 1-1 home draw against Bolton Wanderers during September 2007?

519. In which position in the Premier League did the club finish?

520. Which Jamaican defender did Derby sign in July 2007 from Sheffield United?

LEAGUE GOALSCORERS – 2

Match the player to the number of League goals he scored for Derby County

521.	Jack Parry	22
522.	Mark Pembridge	1
523.	John Hannighan	10
524.	Jim Moore	30
525.	Lee Morris	75
526.	Albert Mays	28
527.	Gordon Hughes	105
528.	Keith Osgood	19
529.	Tommy Johnson	17
530.	Anthony Macken	21

JACOB LAURSEN

531. What nationality is Jacob?

532. True or false: Jacob was part of the team that played in Derby's first ever season in the Premier League?

533. How many League appearances did Jacob make for The Rams in his career – 127, 137 or 147?

534. Against which team did Jacob score for Derby in the 5-2 away win during September 1997?

535. Against which team did Jacob score for Derby in the 3-3 away draw during October 1999 with Rory Delap and Mikkel Beck scoring the other goals for The Rams?

536. Which Derby manager signed Jacob for The Rams in 1996?

537. Following on from the previous question, can you name the other player, a Croatian, the manager signed who was also involved with Croatia in the European Championship Finals?

538. How many League goals did Jacob score for The Rams in his career?

539. Against which team did Jacob score in the 1-1 home draw during September 1996, in only his fourth League appearance for the club?

540. In which season did Jacob win the Derby County Player of the Year award?

CHARLIE GEORGE

541. In which year was Charlie born in London – 1940, 1950 or 1960?

542. How much did Charlie cost Derby County when he signed in 1975?

543. Following on from the previous question, which Derby County manager signed Charlie?

544. How many playing spells did Charlie have at the Baseball Ground?

545. Against which team did Charlie make his League debut for Derby County in August 1975 in a 1-1 away draw?

546. True or false: Charlie scored on his Derby County home debut in August 1975?

547. Charlie finished Derby's highest League scorer in his first season at the Baseball Ground, but with how many goals in his 35 starts – 14, 15 or 16?

548. Against which London club did Charlie score a hat-trick in the 8-2 home win in the League during October 1976 in Division One?

549. Against which club did Charlie score a hat-trick in the 4-2 home win in the League during January 1978 in Division One, with Gerry Daly scoring the other goal for The Rams?

550. How many full England caps did Charlie win for his country?

UEFA CUP

551.   In which year did the club first play in the UEFA Cup?

552.   Can you name the Switzerland team that were Derby's opponents in their first game in this competition?

553.   Following on from the previous question, can you name the player who scored a brace in the 4-1 home win in the first leg in round one?

554.   Who was Derby's manager when they played in this competition for the very first time in their history?

555.   Which Irish team did Derby beat 12-0 at home in the first round, first leg during September 1976?

556.   Following on from the previous question, can you name the player who scored five goals in the game for the Rams?

557.   Following on from the previous question, can you name the two players who scored a hat-trick in the 12-0 home win?

558.   Which Greek club knocked Derby out in the second round, by winning 5-2 on aggregate during October and November 1976?

559.   Which competition did the club first play in during their history – in the European Cup or the UEFA Cup?

560.   Which goalkeeper played in the club's four UEFA matches during the 1976/1977 season?

PREMIER LEAGUE SEASON – 1998/1999

561. Who was Derby's manager during this season?

562. In what position in the Premier League did Derby County finish?

563. True or false: Derby County drew their first three League matches?

564. Which team did Derby County beat during September 1998 to record their first League win of the season with Paulo Wanchope scoring the only goal in a 1-0 home win?

565. Which Derby player scored a brace against Everton at home during February 1999 in a 2-1 win?

566. How many of the club's 38 League games did Derby win – 13, 14 or 15?

567. True or false: Derby County beat Leicester City both at home and away in the League season?

568. Which defender played the opening match of the League season and was then transferred to Blackburn Rovers for £5.35 million?

569. Who was the club's Player of the Season, having made 37 League starts during this season?

570. How many League goals did Horacio Carbonari score for Derby County during this season in his 28 starts and one substitute appearance?

ARTHUR COX

571. In which year was Arthur appointed Derby County manager?

572. Which team did Arthur manage before he joined Derby County as manager?

573. Which position in Division Three did Arthur guide The Rams to in his first season in charge at the Baseball Ground?

574. True or false: Arthur guided the club to promotion to Division Two during his second season at County?

575. Which manager took over from Arthur when he left the club in 1993?

576. Which team did Arthur manage between 1976 and 1980?

577. Which position did Derby finish in the League during 1987/1988 when they played in Division One for the first time during Arthur's managerial time at the club?

578. In which year was Arthur born – 1937, 1938 or 1939?

579. True or false: Arthur won his first League game in charge as Derby County manager?

580. In which season did Arthur guide Derby County to win the Division Two championship?

PAUL SIMPSON

581.   From which club did Derby sign Paul in 1992?

582.   Against which club did Paul score a hat-trick in the 4-3 home defeat during September 1992?

583.   True or false: Paul scored on his Derby League debut away against Leicester City during February 1992?

584.   At which club did Paul start his professional football career, making his debut as a 16-year-old?

585.   How many goals did Paul score in his first season at the Baseball Ground in his 16 starts – five, six or seven?

586.   In which year was Paul born in Carlisle – 1965, 1966 or 1967?

587.   Against which club did Paul score a hat-trick in the 3-0 home win during January 1995?

588.   How many League goals did Paul score in his Derby County career in his 134 starts and 52 substitute appearances – 48, 58 or 68?

589.   How much did Paul cost The Rams when he signed for Derby County?

590.   Which club did Paul join when he left Derby County?

JOHN McGOVERN

591.   In which position did John play for Derby County?

592.   Against which London team did John make his Derby debut during November 1968 in a 2-1 home win?

593.   True or false: John scored on his Rams debut?

594.   How many League goals did John score in his Derby County career – 16, 26 or 36?

595.   Against which team did John score a brace in a 4-2 away League win during August 1970?

596.   Against which team did John score the first goal in a 2-0 home League win during December 1969?

597.   In which year was John born in Montrose – 1947, 1948 or 1949?

598.   Which team did John sign from to join Derby in 1968?

599.   True or false: John won a championship medal in his first season at the Baseball Ground?

600.   How many League appearances did John make in his Derby County career – 190, 290 or 390?

DIVISION TWO CHAMPIONS – 1986/1987

601. Who was County's manager during this success?

602. Can you name one of the three players who played in all 42 League matches?

603. How many of the club's 42 matches did Derby County win – 21, 23 or 25?

604. Which Derby County player won the Player of the Year award?

605. Which team finished in second place in Division Two, six points behind The Rams?

606. Which Derby player finished the club's highest League scorer with 19 goals?

607. True or false: Derby County were unbeaten in the League during March 1987?

608. Who scored County's first League goal of the season in the club's second League game of the season in the 1-1 away draw during August 1986 against Birmingham City?

609. Who scored a hat-trick for The Rams in a 3-0 home win against Reading during December 1986?

610. Which team did The Rams beat on the last day of the League season, a 4-2 home win during May 1987?

DERBY V LEICESTER CITY

611.   The sides first met in February 1894, in which competition were they playing?

612.   Which striker scored Derby's only goal in the 1-0 home win in the Championship during November 2006?

613.   True or false: The sides met in the League, FA Cup and League Cup during the 1960s?

614.   What was the score when the sides met in April 2000 at Pride Park in the Premier League?

615.   Who scored Derby's 89th minute equaliser in the 1-1 home draw in the Premier League during October 2005?

616.   Which Derby player scored the only goal in the 1-0 home win in Division One during December 1976?

617.   Which team finished higher in the Premier League during 1997/1998 – Derby County or Leicester City?

618.   What was the score in the teams first ever meeting in the Premier League, played at the Baseball Ground during November 1996?

619.   Which midfielder scored Derby's 90th minute equaliser in the 1-1 draw at home during March 2003 in the Premier League?

620.   Which Derby player scored a brace in the 2-1 away win at Filbert Street during October 1997 in the Premier League?

LEAGUE POSITIONS – 1

Match the position Derby County finished to the season

621.	2007/2008	6th in Division One
622.	2005/2006	2nd in Division One
623.	2003/2004	20th in the Premier League
624.	2001/2002	16th in Division One
625.	1999/2000	20th in Division One
626.	1997/1998	3rd in Division Two
627.	1995/1996	9th in the Premier League
628.	1993/1994	20th in the Championship
629.	1991/1992	19th in the Premier League
630.	1989/1990	16th in the Premier League

EMANUEL VILLA

631. In what position does Emanuel play?

632. Which Rams manager signed Emanuel for Derby County?

633. Against which team did Emanuel make his Rams debut during January 2008 in a 1-0 home defeat?

634. What squad number did Emanuel wear during the 2008/2009 season?

635. What nationality is Emanuel?

636. Against which team did Emanuel score his first League goal for Derby County, in a 1-1 away draw scoring the equaliser in the 89th minute during February 2008?

637. In which year was Emanuel born – 1980, 1981 or 1982?

638. From which Mexican team did Derby buy Emanuel in 2008?

639. Which team were Derby playing when they drew 2-2 at home during March 2008 with Emanuel scoring a brace in the game?

640. Against which team did Emanuel score a hat-trick in a 5-1 away win in the League Cup 3rd round during November 2008?

GARY MICKLEWHITE

641. How many League goals did Gary score in his Derby County career – 31, 41 or 51?

642. Against which team did Gary score his first League goal for Derby during March 1985 in a 1-1 away draw?

643. Which Derby manager brought Gary for the Rams in 1985?

644. Against which team did Gary score a brace in a 7-0 home win during November 1985?

645. How many League games did Gary play for Derby County in his career – 200, 240 or 280?

646. In which position did Gary play during his playing days?

647. In which year was Gary born in Southwark – 1960, 1961 or 1962?

648. Gary was ever present for Derby during the 1986/1987 season, can you name one of the other two players who played in every game for the Rams?

649. Against which team did Gary score the winning goal in a 2-1 home League win during April 1988?

650. From which London club did Derby County sign Gary in 1985?

DIVISION TWO CHAMPIONS – 1968/1969

651.   Did Derby County win their last 9, 10 or 11 League games?

652.   True or false: Derby failed to win one of their first five League matches?

653.   Who scored the club's only League hat-trick during this season, on the final day of the season in a 5-0 home win against Bristol City in May 1969?

654.   Who played in goal for Derby in all 42 League matches during this season?

655.   Who was Derby County's Player of the Season?

656.   How many of the club's 42 League matches did they win – 26, 27 or 28?

657.   Who finished the club's highest League scorer with 16 goals in 41 starts?

658.   Against which team did Derby record their first win of the season, a 2-0 home win during August 1968 with Roy McFarland and John O'Hare scoring the goals?

659.   Which manager led the club to this success?

660.   Which team did The Rams beat 3-2 at home on Boxing Day 1968 with Alan Hinton scoring a brace and Roy McFarland scoring the goals for Derby?

LEAGUE APPEARANCES – 2

Match the player to the number of League appearances he made for Derby County

661.	Tony Dorigo	51 (7)
662.	Tom Huddlestone	6 (9)
663.	Ralph Hann	7
664.	Paul Kitson	30
665.	John Gregory	115
666.	Mark Lillis	84 (4)
667.	Kevin Lisbie	105
668.	Paul Goddard	37 (4)
669.	John McAlle	103
670.	George Foster	49

2005/2006

671. Who was the Rams manager before Terry Westley took over in January 2006?

672. True or false: Derby drew 20 games out of the 46 League games?

673. Which forward scored the winning goal in the 2-1 home win against Stoke City in the League during October 2005?

674. With which team did Derby draw 1-1 at home on the opening day of the season?

675. Against which club did Derby record their highest League win of the season, a 5-1 home win during January 2006?

676. Following on from the previous question, can you name the Rams player who scored a brace in the game?

677. In which position did the club finish in the Championship?

678. True or false: Derby were unbeaten in the League during August 2005?

679. Who finished the club's highest League scorer with 11 goals in 41 starts and one substitute appearance?

680. How many players did the club use in League matches during this season – 37, 38 or 39?

KEVIN HECTOR

681. What was Kevin's nickname at the Baseball Ground?

682. Which team did Kevin play for before he joined Derby in 1966?

683. Against which club did Kevin make his Rams League debut in September 1966, in a 2-1 away defeat?

684. Kevin finished Derby's highest scorer in his first season at the club, how many goals did he score in his 30 starts – 14, 15 or 16?

685. In which position did Kevin play in his playing career?

686. Which manager brought Kevin back to Derby County is 1980 for his second playing spell at the club?

687. How many Division One championship medals did Kevin win whilst at the Baseball Ground?

688. True or false: Kevin won two full international caps for England?

689. Against which team did Kevin score a hat-trick in a 5-1 away League win during September 1967 with John O'Hare scoring the other two goals for The Rams?

690. How many playing spells did Kevin have at Derby County – two, three or four?

THE LEAGUE CUP

691.   Which top flight team knocked Derby out of the semi-finals during the 2008/2009 season, winning 4-3 on aggregate?

692.   Following on from the previous question, can you name the Derby player who scored the only goal in the 1-0 home win in the first leg during January 2009?

693.   Against which club did Derby play their first ever League Cup game on 11 October 1960, a 5-2 away win in the 1st round?

694.   Who scored a hat-trick in Derby's 3rd round 6-0 win against Sunderland at the Baseball Ground during October 1990?

695.   Which round did the club reach in the 1997/1998 season before being knocked out against Newcastle United in November 1997?

696.   Against which team did Deon Burton score a brace during the 3-0 2nd round home win during September 2001?

697.   Which Yorkshire based team knocked Derby out of the semi-finals during the 1967/1968 season, winning 4-2 on aggregate?

698.   True or false: Derby played West Ham United three times in this competition in the 1989/1990 season?

699.   Which Derby player scored the club's first ever hat-trick in this competition during September 1967 against Hartlepools United in the 2nd round 4-0 win?

700.   Which Derby defender scored the only goal in the 1-0 away win in the 1st round during August 2006?

JIM SMITH

701. In which year was Jim appointed manager of The Rams?

702. True or false: Jim guided the club to second place in Division One in his first season in charge at Derby County?

703. Which future England manager did Jim appoint as his assistant manager when he became manager of The Rams?

704. What was the score in Jim's first League match in charge at Derby County?

705. Which Midlands club did Jim manager between 1978 and 1982?

706. What is Jim's nickname?

707. True or false: Jim played for Derby County in his career?

708. What is Jim's middle name?

709. How many full seasons did Jim manage the club in the Premier League?

710. Which midfielder did Jim sign for The Rams on loan in 1999 and then on a permanent basis for £3 million in April 2001 from Ajax?

PREMIER LEAGUE SEASON – 1997/1998

711.   The club played their first ever match at Pride Park in the 3rd League match of the season, who was the game against in a 1-0 win?

712.   Following on from the previous question, can you name the Rams player who scored the first goal at the stadium?

713.   In which position did Derby finish in the Premier League?

714.   Can you name Derby's goalscorers who scored in the 3-0 home win against Arsenal during November 1997?

715.   Who won the Derby County Player of the Year award, this being in his first season since signing from Italian side Fiorentina?

716.   Which team did Derby beat 1-0 at home on the final day of the season with Paulo Wanchope scoring the only goal?

717.   True or false: Derby were unbeaten in the League during January 1998?

718.   Who scored the only goal in the 1-0 win over West Ham United on Boxing Day 1997 at Pride Park?

719.   How many of the club's 38 League matches did they win – 16, 17 or 18?

720.   Who was Derby's manager during this season?

IGOR STIMAC

721.   What nationality is Igor?

722.   Can you name the London club Igor played for when
       he left Derby County in 1999?

723.   How many League appearances did Igor make for The
       Rams – 74, 84 or 174?

724.   In which year was Igor born?

725.   Against which club did Igor make his Derby League
       debut in November 1995 in a 5-1 away defeat?

726.   True or false: Igor scored for Derby County on his
       League debut?

727.   Which Derby County manager signed Igor for The
       Rams in 1995?

728.   True or false: Igor won the Player of the Season award
       in his second season at Derby County?

729.   Against which club did Igor score his only League goal
       for The Rams during 1996/1997, in a 2-2 home draw
       during February 1997?

730.   Igor scored the first goal for Derby in the 2-1 away win
       against Everton during February 1998, can you name
       the Derby forward who scored the club's winning goal
       in the game?

MART POOM

731. For which country does Mart play international football?

732. Against which team did Mart make his Derby League debut during April 1997 in a 3-2 away win?

733. In which season did Mart win the Player of the Year award at Derby County?

734. Which Rams manger signed Mart for Derby County?

735. Mart played in 36 of Derby's 38 League matches during 1997/1998, which Derby County goalkeeper played in the two games Mart missed during March and April 1998?

736. From which club did Mart sign to join Derby County in 1997?

737. How many League appearances did Mart make for Derby County in his career – 146, 156 or 166?

738. Which team did Mart sign for in May 2007 from Arsenal after making only one League appearance?

739. True or false: Mart once scored a League goal while playing for Sunderland?

740. In which year was Mart born – 1970, 1971 or 1972?

GERAINT WILLIAMS

741.   In which position did Geraint play during his playing
        days?

742.   In which year did Geraint join Derby County?

743.   Following on from the previous question, which club
        did Geraint leave to join County?

744.   How many League goals did Geraint score for Derby
        during 1985/1986?

745.   Against which club did Geraint score his only League
        goal of the 1986/1987 season for Derby County?

746.   Geraint left the Baseball Ground in 1992, which club
        did he join?

747.   For which country did Geraint win 13 full
        international caps?

748.   True or false: Geraint was Derby's Player of the Season
        during 1986/1987?

749.   Against which club did Geraint score his only League
        goal of the 1987/1988 season for Derby County in a
        3-0 away win during March 1988?

750.   Which Essex based team did Geraint play for between
        1998 and 2000 and then managed them between
        2006 and 2008?

DERBY V LEEDS UNITED

751.   True or false: These two sides met in the League during the 1980s?

752.   Can you name Derby's two goalscorers who scored in the 2-1 win in the League Cup 4th round match during November 2008?

753.   True or false: The sides drew both League matches during the 2006/2007 season in the Championship?

754.   What was the score in the League match between the sides at Pride Park during January 2005?

755.   In which year did the sides first meet on 4 March finishing in a 2-1 Leeds win, and then played them a week later and Derby won 2-0 at home?

756.   Which two competitions did the sides meet during the 1995/1996 season?

757.   What was the score when the sides met in Division One at home during March 1970 – 3-1, 4-1 or 5-1?

758.   In which year did the teams first meet in the FA Cup – 1960, 1961 or 1962?

759.   Derby were beating Leeds United 3-0 at Elland Road after 33 minutes in a Premier League match during November 1997, what was the final score in the game?

760.   True or false: Derby played Leeds United on 10 League occasions throughout the 1990s and didn't win one of them?

LEAGUE POSITIONS – 2

Match the position Derby County finished to the season

761.	1987/1988	1st in Division One
762.	1985/1986	16th in Division Two
763.	1983/1984	4th in Division One
764.	1981/1982	20th in Division Two
765.	1979/1980	3rd in Division One
766.	1977/1978	4th in Division One
767.	1975/1976	3rd in Division Three
768.	1973/1974	12th in Division One
769.	1971/1972	15th in Division One
770.	1969/1970	21st in Division One

KEVIN McMINN

771. In which position did Kevin play during his playing career?

772. What nationality is Kevin?

773. Against which club did Kevin make his Rams debut during February 1988 in a 2-1 away defeat?

774. What is Kevin's middle name?

775. True or false: Kevin scored on his Derby home debut against Manchester United in a 2-1 home defeat during February 1988?

776. In which year was Kevin born – 1960, 1961 or 1962?

777. How many League goals did Kevin score in his Derby County career?

778. Which Spanish club did Kevin sign from to join Derby County in 1988?

779. Against which club did Kevin score in a 2-0 home win in Division Two during March 1992?

780. Which Derby manager signed Kevin for the Rams?

LEAGUE APPERANCES – 3

Match the player to the number of League appearances he made for Derby County

781.	Gary Mills	223
782.	John Goodall	245
783.	Lionel Murphy	6
784.	Kevin Ratcliffe	2
785.	Paul Peschisolido	2 (2)
786.	Ben Hall	211
787.	Paul Parker	221
788.	John Howe	4
789.	Avi Nimni	35 (42)
790.	Alan Lewis	18

STEVE POWELL

791. How old was Steve when he made his Derby County debut in the Texaco Cup against Stoke City in October 1971?

792. Following on from the previous question, which Rams manager handed Steve his debut?

793. What was the name of Steve's father who played in 380 League games for the Rams?

794. True or false: Steve won two Division One Championship medals whilst at Derby County?

795. How many League goals did Steve score in his Derby County career – 20, 21 or 22?

796. In which season did Steve win the Player of the Year award whilst at the Baseball Ground?

797. Against which London team did Steve score a brace in a 2-1 home win during February 1975?

798. Against which club did Steve score in a 2-0 away League win during December 1984 with Bobby Davison scoring the other goal for The Rams?

799. Against which club did Steve score in a 2-0 home League win on the final day of the 1973/1974 season?

800. How many League games did Steve play for Derby County in his football career – 360, 361 or 362?

DAVE MACKAY

801. Which club did Dave join Derby County from in 1968?

802. Against which club did Dave make his Derby League debut on the opening day of the 1968/1969 season in a 1-1 away draw?

803. True or false: Dave guided Derby County to the Division One title in only his second season in charge at the club?

804. How many League goals did Dave score for Derby County in his career – three, five or seven?

805. Against which team did Dave score the winning goal in the 3-2 home win during February 1970 with John O'Hare and Kevin Hector scoring the others for The Rams?

806. How many League games did Dave play in for Derby County in his career – 112, 122 or 132?

807. Against which club did Dave score his first Derby County League goal during November 1968 in a 3-3 home draw?

808. How many goals did Dave score for Scotland in his 22 full international caps?

809. In which season did Dave captain Derby County to the Division Two Championship?

810. Who took over as The Rams manager when Dave left the Baseball Ground as manager in 1976?

1990s

811.   Who was the Derby County manager at the start of the decade?

812.   Which team beat the Rams 2-1 in the Division One play-off final in May 1994 at Wembley?

813.   Which team beat the Rams 3-1 in the Anglo-Italian final in May 1993?

814.   Following on from the previous question, who scored Derby's goal in the game?

815.   In which position did Derby finish in Division One during 1992/1993?

816.   Which two players were sold to Aston Villa in 1995 in a joint deal for £2.9 million?

817.   Who was the club's highest League scorer with 13 goals in the 1991/1992 season?

818.   The first 30,000 plus attendance at the new Pride Park stadium was against which team played on 18 October 1997 in a 2-2 draw?

819.   Which Derby midfielder represented the Rams in the 1994 World Cup Finals for USA?

820.   Who was the Derby County manager on 31 December 1999?

PETER TAYLOR

821.   True or false: Peter followed Brian Clough as his
       assistant manager in 1967 to the Baseball Ground?

822.   Which chairman brought Peter back to Derby County
       in 1982 and appointed him as club manager?

823.   Following on from the previous question, which
       manager did Peter take over from as manager of the
       Rams?

824.   Which club did Peter manage between 1962 and
       1965?

825.   At which club were Peter and Brian Clough when they
       met each other and formed a great friendship?

826.   In which position did Peter play during his playing
       days?

827.   How many Division One Championships did Derby win
       whilst Peter was assistant manager to Brian Clough?

828.   Which team did Peter play for between 1955 and
       1961?

829.   What is Peter's middle name?

830.   When Peter was appointed manager of Derby County
       in 1982 which former Rams legend was appointed as
       his assistant?

WHERE DID THEY GO – 2

*Match up the player to the team he joined
after leaving Derby County*

831.   Paul Williams   **Leicester City**

832.   Dean Sturridge   **Sheffield
                              Wednesday**

833.   Jacob Laursen   **Coventry City**

834.   Martin Taylor   **Luton Town**

835.   Ian Ormondroyd   **Wycombe
                              Wanderers**

836.   Phil Gee   **Watford**

837.   Craig Ramage   **Leicester City**

838.   Mickey Lewis   **FC Copenhagen**

839.   Mark Pembridge   **Oxford United**

840.   Mick Harford   **Leicester City**

STEFANO ERANIO

841. For which Italian team did Stefano play before he joined The Rams in 1997?

842. Stefano scored five League goals in his first season at Derby, how many of them were penalties?

843. In which year was Stefano born – 1965, 1966 or 1967?

844. Against which London team did Stefano score in a 2-1 defeat at Pride Park during April 2001?

845. Against which team did Stefano make his Derby County League debut on the opening day of the 1997/1998 season in a 1-0 away defeat?

846. Which Rams manager signed Stefano for Derby County in 1997?

847. How many goals did Stefano score for Italy in his 20 full international caps?

848. Stefano scored his first League goal for Derby County in the Premier League in his third match for the club, which team did he score against during a 1-0 home win during August 1997?

849. Against which club did Stefano score Derby's second goal in the 2-0 home League win during April 2001?

850. How many League appearances did Stefano make for The Rams in his football career – 95, 98 or 101?

DERBY'S FIRST SEASON IN THE PREMIER LEAGUE – 1996/1997

851.   Against which team did Derby play in their first Premier League game on 17 August 1996, finishing in a 3-3 home draw?

852.   Which team did Derby beat 2-1 away in their fifth match of the season during September 1996 to record their first win in the Premier League?

853.   Who was The Rams manager during this season?

854.   True or false: Derby were unbeaten in the League during November 1996?

855.   Which striker scored the winning goal in the 3-2 home win against Chelsea in March 1997?

856.   Dean Sturridge finished the club's highest League scorer this season, but with how many goals?

857.   True or false: Derby beat Manchester United (who finished the season as champions of the Premier League) 3-2 at Old Trafford in April 1997?

858.   Which defender did The Rams sign in October from Aston Villa who went on to make 23 starts and one substitute appearance this season?

859.   How many clean sheets did the club keep in their 38 League matches?

860.   How many points were the club clear of relegation – 6, 16 or 26?

COLIN ADDISON

861. Which Derby chairman appointed Colin manager of The Rams?

862. In which year was Colin appointed manager of Derby County?

863. Which manager did Colin take over from at the Baseball Ground?

864. True or false: Derby were relegated in Colin's first season in charge at the Baseball Ground?

865. In which position in Division Two did Colin guide Derby County during the 1980/1981 season?

866. Against which club did Colin record his highest win as Derby County manager, a 4-0 home win during October 1979?

867. In which year was Colin born in Taunton?

868. What was the score in Colin's first League match in charge at Derby County, against West Bromwich Albion on the opening day of the season?

869. Which team did Derby beat 4-1 at home with Colin in charge, their biggest League win of the 1980/1981 season with Alan Biley and Dave Swindlehurst both scoring braces in the game during Boxing Day 1980?

870. Who was appointed as Derby manager when Colin left the club in 1982?

TIM WARD

871. Which Derby County manager did Tim take over from in 1962?

872. Which player did Tim buy for £10,000 from Cardiff City in July 1963?

873. True or false: The club played in Division Two for the whole time Tim was in charge at the Baseball Ground?

874. In which year was Tim born – 1916, 1917 or 1918?

875. In which position in Division Two did Tim guide the club in his first season at Derby County?

876. Against which club did Derby play their last game with Tim in charge during May 1967, a 1-1 home draw?

877. Tim had to wait until his sixth League match in charge of Derby County until he had his first win, which team did The Rams beat 1-0 at home during September 1962?

878. What is the highest position Tim guided the club to in Division Two during his managerial career at Derby County?

879. How many League goals did Tim score in his 238 appearances at Derby County during his career?

880. Which manager took over from Tim in 1967 when he left the Baseball Ground?

MATCH THE YEAR – 1

Match up the year to the event

881.	Jack Parry scored his 100th League goal for Derby against Swansea Town	2003
882.	Derby won the Charity Shield	2008
883.	Mile Sterjovski was born	1978
884.	Derby lost 7-1 at home to Middlesbrough in Division Two	1973
885.	Paul Connolly joined Derby County from Plymouth Argyle	1963
886.	The club was European Champion Clubs' Cup semi-finalist	1959
887.	John Gregory left the club as manager	1953
888.	Danny Higginbotham was born	1969
889.	The club record their record attendance at the Baseball Ground, 41,826 against Tottenham Hotspur in Division One	1975
890.	Stuart McMillan left the club as manager	1979

PREMIER LEAGUE SEASON – 2000/2001

891. Who was the club's Player of the Season?

892. Malcolm Christie was Derby's highest League scorer, but with how many goals?

893. Who finished Premier League champions during this season?

894. True or false: Derby County won their first League match in their 14th attempt?

895. What was the score when Derby visited Old Trafford during May 2001 against Manchester United?

896. Following on from the previous question, who scored for County?

897. Which team did Derby County play on the opening day of the season, a 2-2 home draw during August 2000?

898. Who was the club's manager during this season?

899. Which Midlands team did Derby County beat 1-0 at home during February 2001 with Deon Burton scoring a penalty?

900. Which East Anglian based team did Derby County draw 1-1 with at home on the last day of the League season with Malcolm Christie scoring The Rams goal?

ARCHIE GEMMILL

901. Against which team did Archie make his Derby County League debut in a 2-1 away defeat during September 1970?

902. How many League games did Archie play for Derby County in his professional football career – 324, 354 or 384?

903. In which year was Archie born in Paisley – 1946, 1947 or 1948?

904. Against which team did Archie score his only League goal during the 1976/1977 season, in a 4-0 home win during April 1977?

905. From which team did Archie sign from in 1970 to join the Rams?

906. How many playing spells did Archie have at the Baseball Ground?

907. Which Derby manager brought Archie back to Derby County for his second spell in 1982?

908. True or false: Archie scored two League goals for Derby County during 1983/1984 and both goals were penalties?

909. How many goals did Archie score in his 43 full international caps for Scotland?

910. In which position did Archie play during his playing days?

MARK WRIGHT

911.   Against which team did Mark score his first League goal for The Rams during December 1987 in a 1-1 home draw?

912.   From which club did Arthur Cox sign Mark for The Rams in 1987?

913.   How many League appearances did Mark make for Derby County in his career – 134, 144 or 154?

914.   Mark scored the first goal in a 2-1 away League win at Manchester United during January 1990, can you name the Rams player who scored Derby's winner in the game?

915.   In which position did Mark play during his playing days?

916.   Against which team did Mark make his Derby County debut in August 1987 in a 1-0 home defeat?

917.   How many full international caps did Mark win for England during his career, scoring one goal?

918.   Which club was Mark appointed manager in 2008 for a third managerial spell at the club?

919.   How much did Mark cost Derby County when he joined The Rams - £740,000, £750,000 or £760,000?

920.   In which year was Mark born in Dorchester-on-Thames?

DARRYL POWELL

921. Which club did Darryl sign from in 1995 to join The Rams?

922. How many League appearances did Darryl make for The Rams in his career – 197, 207 or 217?

923. Against which team did Darryl score in the 2-2 away draw during December 1996 in the Premier League?

924. For which country did Darryl play at full international level during his playing career?

925. Following on from the previous question, which other Derby County player was a part of the international squad that travelled with the 1998 World Cup Squad?

926. In which position did Darryl play during his playing days?

927. Against which team did Darryl score in the 1-1 away draw during February 1996 in Division One?

928. Which Derby manager signed Darryl for the Rams in July 1995?

929. In which year was Darryl born in London – 1970, 1971 or 1972?

930. How many League goals did Darryl score in his Derby County career – 5, 10 or 15?

MATCH THE YEAR – 2

Match up the year to the event

931.	The club won the Watney Cup	2008
932.	Lee Holmes became the youngest player to appear for the Rams aged 15	1974
933.	The record home attendance of 33,378 was recorded at Pride Park against Liverpool	1970
934.	Robbie Savage was born	2003
935.	George Burley left the club as manager	1955
936.	The club was formed	2000
937.	General Sports and Entertainment purchased Derby County Football Club	1996
938.	The club first played Premier League football	1884
939.	Harry Storer became the club's manager	2005
940.	Derby County's academy, Moor Farm, was built	2002

MICHAEL FORSYTH

941. Against which club did Michael score his first Derby County League goal in a 3-2 home win during October 1986?

942. How many League appearances did Michael play for Derby in his career – 325, 326 or 327?

943. Against which club did Michael score for Derby in the League Cup 3rd round in a 2-1 away defeat during October 1991?

944. In which position did Michael play during his playing days?

945. True or false: Michael was one of three players to play in every League match during the 1989/1990 season?

946. In which year was Michael born in Liverpool – 1966, 1967 or 1968?

947. Which club did Michael sign for when he left Derby in 1995?

948. How much did Michael cost Derby from West Bromwich Albion in 1986 - £23,000, £26,000 or £29,000?

949. Which manager signed Michael for Derby County in 1986?

950. How many League goals did Michael score in his Derby County career – Eight, nine or ten?

PREMIER LEAGUE SEASON – 1999/2000

951.   Who was Derby's manager during this season?

952.   With which team did Derby share a 4-4 draw during April 2000 away from home with Craig Burley scoring two penalties for The Rams in the game?

953.   Against which team did Derby record their first League win of the season in their fifth League game during August 1999 in a 2-0 away win?

954.   Who was The Rams top League scorer with eight goals in 34 starts?

955.   How many of the club's 38 League matches did they win?

956.   Who was the club's Player of the Year during this season?

957.   Against which London club did Rory Delap score a brace in a 3-1 home win during October 1999?

958.   Which goalkeeper played in the 10 League matches that Mart Poom missed?

959.   True or false: Derby County were unbeaten in the League during January 2000?

960.   Which team did Derby play on 18 March 2000 and record the then record attendance of 33,378 at Pride Park?

LEAGUE GOALSCORERS – 3

*Match the player to the number of League goals
he scored for Derby County*

961.	Francesco Baiano	11
962.	Mounir El Hamdaoui	15
963.	Sammy Crooks	91
964.	Steven Buckley	35
965.	Bobby Davison	142
966.	Adam Bolder	41
967.	Ian Buxton	101
968.	Leighton James	3
969.	Ron Dix	21
970.	Harry Bedford	16

ROBBIE VAN DER LAAN

971. In which year was Robbie born – 1966, 1967 or 1968?

972. What nationality is Robbie?

973. Which English team did Robbie play for before joining
The Rams?

974. Which Derby manager signed Robbie for The Rams?

975. How many League appearances did Robbie make for
Derby is his career – 65, 85 or 105?

976. Against which Midlands club did Robbie score the
winner in a 2-1 home win during April 1997 in the
Premier League?

977. How many League goals did Robbie score for Derby in
his first season at the club in his 39 starts?

978. Against which team did Robbie make his Derby debut,
on the opening day of the 1995/1996 season in a 0-0
home draw?

979. True or false: Robbie captained the team in his first
season at Derby County?

980. In which year did Robbie leave Derby County and join
Barnsley?

2004/2005

981. Who finished the club's highest League scorer with 16 goals in 35 starts?

982. Which team did Derby County beat 2-1 away from home on Boxing Day 2004?

983. Who scored Derby's first League goal of the season in a 2-1 home defeat to Leicester City during August 2004?

984. True or false: Derby were undefeated in the League during March 2005?

985. Can you name the team that won the Championship during this season?

986. Against which team did Derby record their first win of the season, a 3-2 home win during August 2004?

987. Which goalkeeper played in 45 of the club's 46 League games?

988. Who was Derby's manager during this season?

989. In which position did Derby County finish in the Championship?

990. Which team beat Derby in the play-off semi-finals 2-0 on aggregate?

RON WEBSTER

991.   In which year was Ron born – 1941, 1942 or 1943?

992.   How many managers did Ron play under whilst at County?

993.   Which team did Ron score his only League goal for Derby during the 1971/1972 season in a 3-1 home win?

994.   Which Derby manager handed Ron his Derby County debut in the 1960s?

995.   True or false: Ron was a part of Derby's two Division One Championships successes during the 1970s?

996.   How many League appearances did Ron make his Derby in his career – 455, 460 or 465?

997.   Against which team did Ron score the only winning goal in the 1-0 home win during February 1965?

998.   Which Rams player took Ron's title of making the most senior appearances for Derby County in their history?

999.   How many League goals did Ron score for Derby in his career – 7, 17 or 77?

1000. Which team did Ron score his only League goal for Derby during the 1974/1975 season in a 4-1 home win?

ANSWERS

CLUB RECORDS AND HISTORY

1. *1884*
2. *The Rams*
3. *Manchester United*
4. *Lee Holmes*
5. *Robert Earnshaw*
6. *1972 and 1975*
7. *Once: 1946*
8. *1997*
9. *Brian Clough Trophy*
10. *Kevin Hector*

ROY McFARLAND

11. *Centre half*
12. *1971/1972*
13. *Brian Clough and Peter Taylor*
14. *Malta*
15. *44*
16. *Blackburn Rovers*
17. *Manchester United*
18. *442: 437 (5)*
19. *Seventh*
20. *Four*

NATIONALITIES – 1

21.	*Paulo Wanchope*	*Costa Rican*
22.	*Mark Pembridge*	*Welsh*
23.	*Taribo West*	*Nigerian*
24.	*Paul Peschisolido*	*Canadian*
25.	*Craig Burley*	*Scottish*
26.	*Aljosa Asanovic*	*Croatian*
27.	*Deon Burton*	*Jamaican*
28.	*Peter Shilton*	*English*

| 29. | Stern John | Trinidad & Tobago |
| 30. | Igor Stimac | Croatian |

MARCO GABBIADINI

31.	1968
32.	£1 million
33.	Portsmouth
34.	Six
35.	Southend United
36.	Tranmere Rovers
37.	11
38.	True: Against Sheffield United, Barnsley and Sunderland
39.	14: 5 (9)
40.	Wolves

NICKNAMES – 1

41.	Mr T	Tom Huddlestone
42.	Cat	Chris Powell
43.	Banana	Francesco Baiano
44.	Sticks	Ian Ormondroyd
45.	Rodders	Grzegorz Rasiak
46.	The Pie Man	Marco Gabbiadini
47.	Ray	Gary Charles
48.	Banjo Boy	Deon Burton
49.	Sid	Gordon Cowans
50.	Leaky Bun	Geraint Williams

DIVISION THREE NORTH CHAMPIONS – 1956/1957

51.	Hartlepool United
52.	26
53.	Harry Storer
54.	Gateshead
55.	Ray Straw

56. *True*

57. *False: There were four players that played in 45 matches, therefore all missing one match during the season*

58. *Scunthorpe United*

59. *Three*

60. *True: Derby won four and drew one*

DEAN STURRIDGE

61. *Striker*

62. *1973*

63. *Arthur Cox*

64. *Southend United (away in a 1-0 defeat)*

65. *20*

66. *Leeds United*

67. *Leicester City*

68. *Coventry City*

69. *West Ham United*

70. *Everton*

STADIUMS

71. *Pride Park Stadium*

72. *33,597*

73. *1997*

74. *Wimbledon*

75. *True: During the 1996/1997 season*

76. *1895*

77. *The Osmaston Stand*

78. *Arsenal*

79. *Steve Bloomer*

80. *DE24 8XL*

MANAGERS

81. *Dave Mackey*   *1973*

82.	Billy Davies	2006
83.	Colin Murphy	1976
84.	Arthur Cox	1984
85.	John Gregory	2002
86.	Paul Jewell	2007
87.	Colin Addison	1979
88.	George Burley	2003
89.	Tim Ward	1962
90.	Jim Smith	1995

ROY CARROLL

91.	1977
92.	Goalkeeper
93.	2008
94.	Birmingham City
95.	14
96.	West Ham United
97.	Northern Irish (played for Northern Ireland)
98.	Manchester United
99.	False
100.	Paul Jewell

COLIN BOULTON

101.	Goalkeeper
102.	1945
103.	Tim Ward
104.	Donald
105.	23
106.	1971/1972 and 1974/1975
107.	False
108.	272
109.	True
110.	Bruce Rioch

DIVISION ONE CHAMPIONS – 1971/1972

111. Leeds United

112. Liverpool and Manchester City

113. Brian Clough

114. Colin Todd

115. John McGovern

116. Alan Hinton

117. 16

118. Manchester United

119. Archie Gemmill

120. Frank Wignall

PLAYER OF THE YEAR – 1

121.	2005/2006	Tommy Smith
122.	2003/2004	Youl Mawene
123.	2001/2002	Danny Higginbottom
124.	1993/1994	Martin Taylor
125.	1991/1992	Ted McMinn
126.	1989/1990	Mark Wright
127.	1975/1976	Charlie George
128.	1973/1974	Ron Webster
129.	1971/1972	Colin Todd
130.	1968/1969	Roy McFarland

DERBY V NOTTINGHAM FOREST

131. Emanuel Villa

132. Once: During November 1969 (which was actually a part of the 1969/1970 League season)

133. Grzegorz Rasiak

134. Nottingham Forest: Forest finished 14th and Derby County finished 20th

135. 1-1

136. Horacio Carbonari

137.	True

138.	4-0 to Derby County

139.	Nottingham Forest: Forest finished third and Derby County finished fifth

140.	Paul Peschisolido

SQUAD NUMBERS – 2008/2009

141.	Robbie Savage	8
142.	Jordan Stewart	5
143.	Rob Hulse	11
144.	Andy Todd	22
145.	Mohammed Camara	30
146.	Darren Powell	32
147.	Paul Connolly	2
148.	Mile Sterjovski	16
149.	Dean Leacock	17
150.	Paul Green	4

SPONSORS

151.	Derbyshire Building Society	2005
152.	Bass Brewers	1984
153.	Bombardier	2008
154.	Auto Windscreens	1992
155.	EDS	1998
156.	Puma	1995
157.	Patrick	1981
158.	British Midland	1980
159.	Marston's Pedigree	2001
160.	Sportsweek	1986

STEVE BLOOMER

161.	Two

162.	1912 (1911/1912 season)

163. Stoke

164. 474

165. Inside Right

166. 293

167. Middlesbrough

168. Six

169. 23

170. True: He scored 28 goals in 23 matches

WHERE DID THEY GO – 1

171.	Craig Fagan	Hull City
172.	Paulo Wanchope	West Ham United
173.	Robert Earnshaw	Nottingham Forest
174.	Dean Yates	Watford
175.	Andy Griffin	Stoke City
176.	Christian Dailly	Blackburn Rovers
177.	Grzegorz Rasiak	Tottenham Hotspur
178.	Aljosa Asanovic	Napoli
179.	Fabrizio Ravanelli	Dundee
180.	Rob Lee	West Ham United

WHO AM I? – 1

181. Dean Sturridge

182. Roger Jones

183. Geoff Barrowcliffe

184. Stuart McMillan

185. Horacio Carbonari

186. Tommy Johnson

187. Reg Matthews

188. Frank Upton

189. Jordan Stewart

190. Rob Hulse

1960s

191. Harry Storer
192. 2-0 to Derby County
193. Willie Carlin
194. Kevin Hector
195. 1966/1967
196. Division Two
197. Kevin Hector
198. True
199. Reg Matthews
200. Jack Parry

NICKNAMES – 2

201.	Ace	Aljosa ASanovic
202.	Solly	John O'Hare
203.	Choppy	Paulo Wanchope
204.	Bazooka	Horacio Carbonari
205.	Jug Ears	Rory Delap
206.	Parsley	Mel Sage
207.	Brooklyn	Lee Morris
208.	Sethlad	Seth Johnson
209.	Cracker	Jacob Laursen
210.	Taffy	Leighton James

WHERE DID THEY COME FROM – 1

211.	Paul Connolly	Plymouth Argyle
212.	Paul McGrath	Aston Villa
213.	Terry Hennessey	Nottingham Forest
214.	Gary Rowett	Everton
215.	Russell Hoult	Leicester City
216.	Lewis Price	Ipswich Town
217.	Rob Hulse	Sheffield United
218.	Rory Delap	Carlisle United

219.	Alan Stubbs	Everton
220.	Deon Burton	Portsmouth

1970s

221. Seventh

222. Tottenham Hotspur

223. Francis Lee, Kevin Hector and Bruce Rioch

224. Archie Gemmill

225. Eight

226. Ron Webster

227. Tommy Docherty

228. Wolves

229. Roger Davies

230. David Langan

2008/2009

231. January

232. Sheffield United

233. Coventry City

234. Paul Green, Rob Hulse and Przemyslaw Kazmierczak

235. Martin Albrechtsen

236. Rob Hulse

237. Bristol City

238. Nathan Ellington

239. Rob Hulse

240. True: Derby beat Norwich 2-1 away and then 3-1 at home (both games played in October 2008)

FOUR OR FIVE GOALS IN A GAME

241. Paul Kitson

242. Steve Bloomer

243. Bruce Rioch

244. True

245.   5-1 to Derby County

246.   Division Three North

247.   Alexander Higgins

248.   Division One

249.   True

250.   Roger Davies

LEAGUE APPEARANCES – 1

251.   Frank Wignall   29 (16)

252.   John Robertson   72

253.   Ian Ashbee   1

254.   Lars Bohinen   47 (9)

255.   Taribo West   18

256.   Nigel Callaghan   88

257.   Eric Steele   47

258.   Mark Stallard   19 (8)

259.   John Sims   2 (1)

260.   Malcolm Christie   90 (26)

ALAN HINTON

261.   On the right

262.   1942

263.   £30,000

264.   1967

265.   Rotherham United

266.   Six

267.   Ipswich Town

268.   253: 240 (13)

269.   15

270.   Huddersfield Town

EUROPEAN CUP

271.   1972

272.   Kevin Hector

273.   Brian Clough (1972/1973) and Dave Mackay (1975/1976)

274.   False: The club haven't ever won this competition

275.   Real Madrid

276.   Charlie George (against Real Madrid in October 1975)

277.   Colin Boulton

278.   4-1 (home win in October 1975 in the 2nd round, 1st leg)

279.   Juventus

280.   FK Zeljeznicar Sarajevo (during September 1972)

PREMIER LEAGUE – 2001/2002

281.   True: Two players played in 37 games (Chris Riggott and Danny Higginbotham)

282.   Youl Mawene

283.   Fabrizio Ravanelli and Malcolm Christie

284.   Bolton Wanderers

285.   Sunderland

286.   Lee Morris

287.   Three (four if you include Billy McEwan who also stood in for a very short period)

288.   Jim Smith, Colin Todd and John Gregory

289.   30

290.   Fabrizio Ravanelli

HONOURS

291.	FA Cup Winners	1946
292.	Charity Shield Winners	1975
293.	Division One Champions	1972
294.	Anglo-Italian Cup Runners-Up	1993
295.	Championship Play-Off Winners	2007
296.	Division One Runners-Up	1936
297.	FA Cup Runners-Up	1903
298.	Texaco Cup Winners	1972

| 299. | Watney Cup Winners | 1971 |
| 300. | Division One Champions | 1975 |

NATIONALITIES – 2

301.	Lars Bohinen	Norwegian
302.	Branko Strupar	Belgian
303.	Grzegorz Rasiak	Polish
304.	Marino Rahmberg	Swedish
305.	Rory Delap	Republic of Ireland
306.	John Harkes	American
307.	Avi Nimni	Israeli
308.	Jacob Laursen	Danish
309.	Mart Poom	Estonian
310.	Simo Valakari	Finnish

DIVISION ONE RUNNERS-UP – 1995/1996

311. Four

312. Jim Smith

313. Dean Strurridge

314. True

315. Tranmere Rovers

316. Paul Simpson

317. 21

318. Luton Town

319. Norwich City

320. Russell Hoult (40) and Steve Sutton (6)

NIGEL CLOUGH

321. True: from 1996-1998

322. 14

323. Queens Park Rangers

324. Liverpool

325. 1966

326. Howard
327. Burton Albion
328. Paul Jewell
329. 1989 and 1990 (with Nottingham Forest)
330. Manchester United

BRIAN CLOUGH

331. 1967 (July)
332. Division Two Championship in 1968/1969
333. David Nish
334. Middlesbrough
335. True: Two caps
336. Striker
337. Nottingham Forest
338. Texaco Cup
339. Brighton & Hove Albion
340. Semi-finals

DIVISION ONE CHAMPIONS – 1974/1975

341. Dave Mackay
342. Carlisle United
343. 21
344. Liverpool and Ipswich Town
345. Peter Daniel
346. Colin Boulton and Bruce Rioch
347. False: They won five and lost one (2-1 defeat at home to Stoke City)
348. Sheffield United
349. Kevin Hector
350. Bruce Ricoh

LEAGUE GOALSCORERS - 1

351. Luciano Zavagno   3

352.	Ray Swallow	21
353.	Marcus Tudgay	17
354.	George Thornewell	23
355.	Jack Stamps	100
356.	Jackie Whitehouse	82
357.	Igor Stimac	3
358.	Frank Wignall	15
359.	Dean Saunders	42
360.	Marco Reich	7

TOMMY JOHNSON

361.	1971
362.	£1.375 million
363.	Swindon Town
364.	Eight
365.	Arthur Cox
366.	Port Vale
367.	Aston Villa
368.	98: 91 (7)
369.	Seven
370.	Notts County

THE FA CUP

371.	Steve Davies
372.	Jeff Chandler
373.	Manchester United
374.	Archie Gemmill
375.	1898, 1899 and 1903
376.	True
377.	Aston Villa
378.	Sheffield Wednesday
379.	Charlton Athletic
380.	Jack Stamps

BRUCE RIOCH

381.	Birmingham City
382.	38
383.	Newcastle United
384.	15
385.	Norwich City
386.	Midfielder
387.	24
388.	False
389.	£200,000
390.	Dave Mackay

DEAN SAUNDERS

391.	True
392.	Wimbledon
393.	Arthur Cox
394.	14
395.	Cambridge United
396.	Everton
397.	42
398.	Liverpool
399.	Southampton
400.	True

PLAYER OF THE YEAR – 2

401.	2004/2005	Inigo Idiakez
402.	2000/2001	Chris Riggott
403.	1999/2000	Mart Poom
404.	1997/1998	Francesco Baiano
405.	1990/1991	Dean Saunders
406.	1987/1988	Michael Forsyth
407.	1984/1985	Bobby Davison
408.	1982/1983	Steve Cherry

| 409. | 1979/1980 | Steve Buckley |
| 410. | 1970/1971 | Dave Mackay |

PETER SHILTON

411. 175
412. Southampton
413. Luton Town
414. 125
415. True
416. Arthur Cox
417. Goalkeeper
418. Leslie
419. Plymouth Argyle
420. 47

COLIN TODD

421. Sunderland
422. 1971/1972
423. Central defender (sometimes played in midfield)
424. 2001/2002: from October 2001 until January 2002
425. PFA Players' Player of the Year
426. 27
427. Arsenal
428. Two
429. Everton
430. 1948

LEGENDS

431. Henry Newton
432. Jack Nicholas
433. George Collin
434. Colin Todd
435. Ray Young

436. Reg Harrison

437. Paul Simpson

438. Peter Daniel

439. Gary Micklewhite

440. Bill Curry

FRANCIS LEE

441. Dave Mackay

442. Manchester City

443. £100,000

444. Everton

445. True: Against Coventry City in a 1-1 draw

446. 12

447. Leicester City

448. Striker

449. Sheffield United

450. 10

MIDDLE NAMES

451.	Peter Doherty	Dermont
452.	Charlie Morris	Richard
453.	Bruce Rioch	David
454.	Darryl Powell	Anthony
455.	David Nish	John
456.	Reg Matthews	Derrick
457.	John McGovern	Prescott
458.	Roy McFarland	Leslie
459.	Peter Daniel	Aylmer
460.	Francis Lee	Henry

THE CHAMPIONSHIP PLAY-OFF WINNERS – 2006/2007

461. West Bromwich Albion

462. 1-0

463. **Stephen Pearson**

464. **Stephen Bywater**

465. **74,993**

466. **Southampton**

467. **Billy Davies**

468. **Third**

469. **Two**

470. **Leeds United**

PLAYER POSITIONS

471. **Paul Connolly**   **Defender**

472. **Simon Coleman**   **Defender**

473. **Georgiou Kinkladze**   **Midfielder**

474. **Adam Bolder**   **Midfielder**

475. **Rob Hulse**   **Striker**

476. **Igor Stimac**   **Defender**

477. **Mile Sterjovski**   **Midfielder**

478. **Cyril Fox**   **Goalkeeper**

479. **Brian Launders**   **Midfielder**

480. **Liam Dickinson**   **Striker**

1980s

481. **Fifth**

482. **12**

483. **Kevin Wilson**

484. **Mark Wright**

485. **Andy Garner**

486. **1987**

487. **John Gregory**

488. **Bobby Davison**

489. **They won the Central League**

490. **John Newman**

WHO AM I? – 2

491.   Dean Saunders

492.   Kris Commons

493.   Kevin Hector

494.   Roy McFarland

495.   Phil Brown

496.   Marco Gabbiadini

497.   Martin Albrechtsen

498.   Christopher Riggott

499.   Rod Thomas

500.   Steve Bloomer

WHERE DID THEY COME FROM – 2

501.	Eddie Lewis	Leeds United
502.	Paul Boertien	Carlisle United
503.	Kenny Miller	Celtic
504.	Branko Strupar	Genk
505.	Matt Oakley	Southampton
506.	Craig Short	Notts County
507.	Dean Leacock	Fulham
508.	Danny Higginbotham	Manchester United
509.	David Jones	Manchester United
510.	Warren Barton	Newcastle United

2007/2008

511.   Billy Davies

512.   Robbie Savage

513.   One

514.   Portsmouth

515.   Newcastle United

516.   Kenny Miller

517.   Giles Barnes and Kenny Miller

518.   Kenny Miller

519.   20th
520.   Claude Davis

LEAGUE GOALSCORERS – 2

521.   Jack Parry   105
522.   Mark Pembridge   28
523.   John Hannighan   19
524.   Jim Moore   75
525.   Lee Morris   17
526.   Albert Mays   21
527.   Gordon Hughes   22
528.   Keith Osgood   10
529.   Tommy Johnson   30
530.   Anthony Macken   1

JACOB LAURSEN

531.   Danish
532.   True: during the 1996/1997 season
533.   137: 135 (2)
534.   Sheffield Wednesday
535.   Southampton
536.   Jim Smith
537.   Aljosa Asanovic
538.   Three
539.   Manchester United
540.   1998/1999

CHARLIE GEORGE

541.   1950
542.   £100,000
543.   Dave Mackay
544.   Two
545.   Sheffield United

546. *True*

547. *16*

548. *Tottenham Hotspur*

549. *Coventry City*

550. *One*

UEFA CUP

551. *1974*

552. *Servette Geneva*

553. *Kevin Hector*

554. *Dave Mackay*

555. *Finn Harps*

556. *Kevin Hector*

557. *Charlie George and Leighton James*

558. *AEK Athens*

559. *European Cup, the club played in the European Cup in 1972 and they first played in the UEFA Cup in 1974*

560. *Graham Moseley*

PREMIER LEAGUE SEASON – 1998/1999

561. *Jim Smith*

562. *Eighth*

563. *True*

564. *Sheffield Wednesday*

565. *Deon Burton*

566. *13*

567. *True: Derby won 2-0 at home and 2-1 away*

568. *Christian Dailly*

569. *Jacob Laursen*

570. *Five*

ARTHUR COX

571. *1984*

572. **Newcastle United**

573. **Seventh**

574. **True: The club finished third in Division Three and were promoted**

575. **Roy McFarland**

576. **Chesterfield**

577. **15th**

578. **1939**

579. **False: He lost 1-0 away to Bournemouth on the opening day of the 1984/1985 season**

580. **1986/1987**

PAUL SIMPSON

581. **Oxford United**

582. **Bristol City**

583. **True**

584. **Manchester City**

585. **Seven**

586. **1966**

587. **Portsmouth**

588. **48**

589. **£500,000**

590. **Wolves**

JOHN McGOVERN

591. **Midfield**

592. **Charlton Athletic**

593. **False**

594. **16**

595. **Wolves**

596. **Newcastle United**

597. **1949**

598. **Hartlepools United**

599.   True: Derby won the Division Two title

600.   190: 186 (4)

DIVISION TWO CHAMPIONS – 1986/1987

601.   Arthur Cox

602.   John Gregory, Ross MacLaren and Gary Micklewhite

603.   25

604.   Geraint Williams

605.   Portsmouth

606.   Bobby Davison

607.   True: Three wins and two draws

608.   John Gregory

609.   Bobby Davison

610.   Plymouth Argyle

DERBY V LEICESTER CITY

611.   The FA Cup (0-0 away draw and then Derby won 3-0 in the replay)

612.   Jonathan Stead

613.   False: The teams never met during the 1960s in any competition

614.   3-0 to Derby County

615.   Mounir El Hamdaoui

616.   Leighton James

617.   Derby County: The Rams finished in 9th place and Leicester finished 10th

618.   2-0 to Derby County

619.   Craig Burley

620.   Francesco Baiano

LEAGUE POSITIONS – 1

621.   2007/2008   20th in the Premier League

622.   2005/2006   20th in the Championship

623.	2003/2004	20th in Division One
624.	2001/2002	19th in the Premier League
625.	1999/2000	16th in the Premier League
626.	1997/1998	9th in the Premier League
627.	1995/1996	2nd in Division One
628.	1993/1994	6th in Division One
629.	1991/1992	3rd in Division Two
630.	1989/1990	16th in Division One

EMANUEL VILLA

631. Striker
632. Paul Jewell
633. Wigan Athletic
634. 10
635. Argentinean
636. Birmingham City
637. 1982
638. Tecos (Club de Fútbol Universidad Autónoma de Guadalajara)
639. Fulham
640. Brighton & Hove Albion

GARY MICKLEWHITE

641. 31
642. Brentford
643. Arthur Cox
644. Lincoln City
645. 240: 223 (17)
646. Midfield
647. 1961
648. John Gregory and Ross MacLaren
649. Newcastle United
650. Queens Park Rangers

DIVISION TWO CHAMPIONS – 1968/1969

651. Nine

652. True: Derby drew three and lost two

653. Alan Durban

654. Les Green

655. Roy McFarland

656. 26

657. Kevin Hector

658. Oxford United

659. Brian Clough

660. Middlesbrough

LEAGUE APPEARANCES – 2

661.	Tony Dorigo	37 (4)
662.	Tom Huddlestone	84 (4)
663.	Ralph Hann	115
664.	Paul Kitson	105
665.	John Gregory	103
666.	Mark Lillis	6 (9)
667.	Kevin Lisbie	7
668.	Paul Goddard	49
669.	John McAlle	51 (7)
670.	George Foster	30

2005/2006

671. Phil Brown

672. True

673. Paul Peschisolido

674. Brighton & Hove Albion

675. Crewe Alexandra

676. Tommy Smith

677. 20th

678. False: Derby won two, drew three and lost one

679.   Inigo Idiakez

680.   37

KEVIN HECTOR

681.   The King

682.   Bradford Park Avenue

683.   Crystal Palace

684.   16

685.   Striker

686.   Colin Addison

687.   Two: In 1971/1972 and 1974/1975

688.   True

689.   Cardiff City

690.   Two: 1966-1977 and 1980-1982

THE LEAGUE CUP

691.   Manchester United

692.   Kris Commons

693.   Watford

694.   Mick Harford

695.   4th round

696.   Hull City

697.   Leeds United

698.   True: In the 5th round which ended in a 1-1 away draw and
        then two replays (first replay ended 0-0 at home and second
        replay was won by West Ham United 2-1 away)

699.   John O'Hare

700.   Michael Johnson

JIM SMITH

701.   1995

702.   True

703.   Steve McClaren

704. *0-0: against Port Vale on 13 August 1995*

705. *Birmingham City*

706. *The Bald Eagle*

707. *False*

708. *Michael*

709. *Five: 1996/1997, 1997/1998, 1998/1999, 1999/2000 and 2000/2001 (he did manage Derby until October 2001 so only for a part of 2001/2002)*

710. *Georgi Kinkladze*

PREMIER LEAGUE SEASON – 1997/1998

711. *Barnsley*

712. *Stefano Eranio*

713. *Ninth*

714. *Paulo Wanchope (2) and Dean Sturridge*

715. *Francesco Baiano*

716. *Liverpool*

717. *True: Derby played three matches, they won two and drew one*

718. *Stefano Eranio*

719. *16*

720. *Jim Smith*

IGOR STIMAC

721. *Croatian*

722. *West Ham United*

723. *84*

724. *1967*

725. *Tranmere Rovers*

726. *True*

727. *Jim Smith*

728. *False*

729. *Sheffield Wednesday*

730. *Paulo Wanchope*

MART POOM

731.   *Estonia*

732.   *Manchester United*

733.   *1999/2000*

734.   *Jim Smith*

735.   *Russell Hoult*

736.   *Portsmouth*

737.   *146: 143 (3)*

738.   *Watford*

739.   *True*

740.   *1972*

GERAINT WILLIAMS

741.   *Midfield*

742.   *1985*

743.   *Bristol Rovers*

744.   *Four*

745.   *Stoke City*

746.   *Ipswich Town*

747.   *Wales*

748.   *True*

749.   *Coventry City*

750.   *Colchester United*

DERBY V LEEDS UNITED

751.   *True: During three seasons in the 1980s: 1982/1983,*
       1983/1984, 1986/1987

752.   *Emanuel Villa and Nathan Ellington*

753.   *False: Derby won both matches, 2-0 at home and 1-0 away*

754.   *2-0 to Derby County*

755.   *1922*

756.   *In the he FA Cup and League Cup*

757.   *4-1 to Derby County*

758.   1962 (in January)

759.   4-3 to Leeds United

760.   True: Four draws and six defeats

LEAGUE POSITIONS – 2

761.	1987/1988	15th in Division One
762.	1985/1986	3rd in Division Three
763.	1983/1984	20th in Division Two
764.	1981/1982	16th in Division Two
765.	1979/1980	21st in Division One
766.	1977/1978	12th in Division One
767.	1975/1976	4th in Division One
768.	1973/1974	3rd in Division One
769.	1971/1972	1st in Division One
770.	1969/1970	4th in Division One

KEVIN McMINN

771.   Midfield

772.   Scottish

773.   Portsmouth

774.   Clifton

775.   True

776.   1962

777.   Nine

778.   Sevilla

779.   Plymouth Argyle

780.   Arthur Cox

LEAGUE APPERANCES – 3

781.	Gary Mills	18
782.	John Goodall	211
783.	Lionel Murphy	221
784.	Kevin Ratcliffe	6

785.	Paul Peschisolido	35 (42)
786.	Ben Hall	245
787.	Paul Parker	4
788.	John Howe	223
789.	Avi Nimni	2 (2)
790.	Alan Lewis	2

STEVE POWELL

791. 16
792. Brian Clough
793. Tommy Powell
794. True: In 1971/1972 and 1974/1975
795. 20
796. 1978/1979
797. Arsenal
798. Cambridge United
799. Wolves
800. 362

DAVE MACKAY

801. Tottenham Hotspur
802. Blackburn Rovers
803. True
804. Five
805. Arsenal
806. 122
807. Carlisle United
808. Four
809. 1968/1969
810. Colin Murphy

1990s

811. Arthur Cox

812.	Leicester City
813.	US Cremonese
814.	Marco Gabbiadini
815.	Eighth
816.	Gary Charles and Tommy Johnson
817.	Paul Williams
818.	Manchester United
819.	John Harkes
820.	Jim Smith

PETER TAYLOR

821.	True
822.	Mike Watterson
823.	John Newman
824.	Burton Albion
825.	Middlesbrough
826.	Goalkeeper
827.	One: 1971/1972
828.	Middlesbrough
829.	Thomas
830.	Roy McFarland

WHERE DID THEY GO – 2

831.	Paul Williams	Coventry City
832.	Dean Sturridge	Leicester City
833.	Jacob Laursen	FC Copenhagen
834.	Martin Taylor	Wycombe Wanderers
835.	Ian Ormondroyd	Leicester City
836.	Phil Gee	Leicester City
837.	Craig Ramage	Watford
838.	Mickey Lewis	Oxford United
839.	Mark Pembridge	Sheffield Wednesday
840.	Mick Harford	Luton Town

STEFANO ERANIO

841.   AC Milan

842.   Four

843.   1966

844.   Arsenal

845.   Blackburn Rovers

846.   Jim Smith

847.   Three

848.   Barnsley

849.   Leicester City

850.   95: 83 (12)

DERBY'S FIRST SEASON IN THE PREMIER LEAGUE – 1996/1997

851.   Leeds United

852.   Blackburn Rovers

853.   Jim Smith

854.   True: They played four games, they won three and drew one

855.   Ashley Ward

856.   11

857.   True

858.   Paul McGrath

859.   Seven

860.   6 points: Derby finished on 46 points and Sunderland who finished in 18th place finished with 40 points (other relegated teams were Middlesbrough on 39 points and Nottingham Forest on 34 points)

COLIN ADDISON

861.   George Hardy

862.   1979

863.   Tommy Docherty

864.   True

865.   Sixth

866.	Bolton Wanderers
867.	1940
868.	0-0
869.	Oldham Athletic
870.	John Newman

TIM WARD

871.	Harry Storer
872.	Alan Durban
873.	True
874.	1917
875.	18th
876.	Plymouth Argyle
877.	Preston North End
878.	Eighth: During 1965/1966
879.	Four
880.	Brian Clough

MATCH THE YEAR – 1

881.	Jack Parry scored his 100th League goal for Derby against Swansea Town	1963
882.	Derby won the Charity Shield	1975
883.	Mile Sterjovski was born	1979
884.	Derby lost 7-1 at home to Middlesbrough in Division Two	1959
885.	Paul Connolly joined Derby County from Plymouth Argyle	2008
886.	The club was European Champion Clubs' Cup semi-finalist	1973
887.	John Gregory left the club as manager	2003
888.	Danny Higginbotham was born	1978

| 889. | The club record their record attendance at the Baseball Ground, 41,826 against Tottenham Hotspur in Division One | 1969 |
| 890. | Stuart McMillan left the club as manager | 1953 |

PREMIER LEAGUE SEASON – 2000/2001

891. Chris Riggott

892. Eight

893. Manchester United

894. True: Against Bradford City

895. 1-0 to Derby County

896. Malcolm Christie

897. Southampton

898. Jim Smith

899. Aston Villa

900. Ipswich Town

ARCHIE GEMMILL

901. West Bromwich Albion

902. 324

903. 1947

904. Manchester City

905. Preston North End

906. Two: 1970-1977 and 1982-1984

907. Peter Taylor

908. True: against Newcastle United at home and Blackburn Rovers at home

909. Eight

910. Midfielder

MARK WRIGHT

911. Watford

912. Southampton

913. 144

914. Nick Pickering

915. Centre back

916. Wimbledon

917. 45

918. Chester City

919. £760,000

920. 1963

DARRYL POWELL

921. Portsmouth

922. 207: 187 (20)

923. Arsenal

924. Jamaica

925. Deon Burton

926. Midfielder

927. Grimsby Town

928. Jim Smith

929. 1971

930. 10

MATCH THE YEAR – 2

931.	The club won the Watney Cup	1970
932.	Lee Holmes became the youngest player to appear for the Rams aged 15	2002
933.	The record home attendance of 33,378 was recorded at Pride Park against Liverpool	2000
934.	Robbie Savage was born	1974
935.	George Burley left the club as manager	2005
936.	The club was formed	1884
937.	General Sports and Entertainment purchased Derby County Football Club	2008
938.	The club first played Premier League football	1996

939.	Harry Storer became the club's manager	1955
940.	Derby County's academy, Moor Farm, was built	2003

MICHAEL FORSYTH

941.	Sunderland
942.	325: 323 (2)
943.	Oldham Athletic
944.	Left back
945.	True: Dean Saunders and Geraint Williams were the others
946.	1966
947.	Notts County
948.	£26,000
949.	Arthur Cox
950.	Eight

PREMIER LEAGUE SEASON – 1999/2000

951.	Jim Smith
952.	Bradford City
953.	Sheffield Wednesday
954.	Gary Rowett
955.	Nine
956.	Mart Poom
957.	Chelsea
958.	Russell Hoult
959.	True: The club played three games, they won two and drew one
960.	Liverpool

LEAGUE GOALSCORERS – 3

961.	Francesco Baiano	16
962.	Mounir El Hamdaoui	3
963.	Sammy Crooks	101
964.	Steven Buckley	21
965.	Bobby Davison	91

966.	Adam Bolder	11
967.	Ian Buxton	41
968.	Leighton James	15
969.	Ron Dix	35
970.	Harry Bedford	142

ROBBIE VAN DER LAAN

971. 1968

972. Dutch

973. Port Vale

974. Jim Smith

975. 65: 61 (4)

976. Aston Villa

977. Six

978. Port Vale

979. True

980. 1998

2004/2005

981. Grzegorz Rasiak

982. Wigan Athletic

983. Marcus Tudgay

984. True: Played three, won one and drew two

985. Sunderland

986. Nottingham Forest

987. Lee Camp

988. George Burley

989. Fourth

990. Preston North End

RON WEBSTER

991. 1943

992. Eight

993. *Manchester City*

994. *Tim Ward*

995. *True*

996. *455*

997. *Cardiff City*

998. *Kevin Hector*

999. *Seven*

1000. *Chelsea*

NOTES:

NOTES:

NOTES:

NOTES:

NOTES:

NOTES:

NOTES:

NOTES:

NOTES:

www.apexpublishing.co.uk